The Soviet Union,
the Communist Movement,
and the World

The Soviet Union, the Communist Movement, and the World

PRELUDE TO THE COLD WAR, 1917–1941

Alan J. Levine

PRAEGER

New York
Westport, Connecticut
London

Library of Congress Cataloging-in-Publication Data

Levine, Alan J.
    The Soviet Union, the communist movement, and the world : prelude
to the Cold War, 1917–1941 / Alan J. Levine.
        p. cm.
    Includes bibliographical references.
    ISBN 0–275–93443–8 (alk. paper)
    1. Soviet Union—Politics and government—20th century.
2. Communism—Soviet Union. I. Title.
DK246.L48   1990
947.084—dc20   89–16335

Library of Congress Catalog Card Number: 89–16335
ISBN: 0–275–93443–8

First published in 1990

Praeger Publishers, One Madison Avenue, New York, NY 10010
A division of Greenwood Press, Inc.

Printed in the United States of America

∞

The paper used in this book complies with the Permanent
Paper Standard issued by the National Information Standards
Organization (Z39.48–1984).

10 9 8 7 6 5 4 3 2 1

Contents

The Soviet Union,
the Communist Movement,
and the World

Marxism and Leninism

The cold war between the Soviet Union and the Western democracies is usually regarded as having begun only in 1945. Although that struggle became the central fact of world politics in the 1940s, it had a long prehistory. It can be fully understood only by examining the doctrine and practices of the Soviet Union and the world Communist movement, which had developed long before World War II. The cold war had its origin in the development of a totalitarian Communist regime in the former Russian empire under the shattering impact of World War I.

The guiding doctrine of the Soviet Union and all latter Communist governments was developed by V. I. Lenin, who gave a peculiar twist to the ideas of Marxist socialism. Contrary to a widespread belief carefully fostered by the Communists and also, for obscure reasons, by the Western mass media, it is incorrect to describe modern communism simply as "Marxism." Certainly until the 1950s many Western democratic socialists considered themselves Marxists, and their claim to Marxism was at least as good as that of the Communists. It was not the ideas of Marx but those of Lenin that led to the development of modern totalitarianism. Marx's doctrine of "scientific socialism" did, however, form the foundation and starting point for Lenin.

Socialist ideas had developed in nineteenth-century Europe under the impact of the Industrial Revolution. Karl Marx, a German socialist activist and scholar who spent much of his life in exile in Britain, claimed to base his version of socialism on a scientific analysis of society. Socialism was not merely a moral and political aim but a development toward which society was inevitably heading. Marx fused socialism with Hegelian philosophy and the radical myth of the French Revolution, which had already had a strong influence on the socialist movement. For Marx and for later revolutionaries who seized power in Russia, the French Revolution was a paradigm, or model, of social and political revolution. They glossed over both its atrocities and ultimate failure. Marx interpreted that event, not as a failed attempt to overthrow absolutism, but as an archetypal social transformation from feudalism to capitalism in which the rule of the landed aristocracy was replaced by that of the bourgeoisie. An analogous change would replace the rule of the capitalist property owner by that of the working class or, as Marx called it, the proletariat. Marx and his followers minutely analyzed the details of the French Revolution as the model of revolutionary change, and Victorian British society as the archetype of a capitalist society.

Marx's interpretation of history was one of extreme economic determinism. Labor, which Marx generally interpreted as meaning only the work of the lowest social class, was the only source or measure of value. History was a dialectical process whose "motor" was the change in the means of economic production (which caused all major historical events) and the struggle between social classes. Marx outlined a simplistic unilinear scheme to describe the evolution of society. Humanity proceeded from a state of primitive communism, where the means of production, such as they were, were collectively owned, to a slave-based society, thence to feudalism, capitalism, and finally to the utopia of communism, in which social classes would finally be abolished. Capitalism would cause its own destruction; its basic characteristics would culminate in an overwhelming concentration of wealth in the hands of a few, while the exploited mass of workers would be progressively impoverished and driven to revolt. A "dictatorship of the proletariat" would result, and the world would return to a collectivist order.

It should be noted that Marx was probably aware that not all societies fitted fully into this unilinear pattern of evolution. He was a firm believer in the superiority of the white race and maintained that the pattern outlined in *Das Kapital* applied to the countries inhabited by Europeans and their descendants—not necessarily to other parts of the world. But his followers overlooked Marx's qualifications and treated his work as applicable to the whole globe. Marx failed to detail either the precise nature of the future socialist order or the exact steps by which it would be formed. He never actually defined the phrase "dictatorship of the proletariat"; in his later years he appears to have believed that it would mean no greater suppression of liberty than in an ordinary "bourgeois" republic. He suggested that, at least in the English-speaking countries and the Netherlands, the transition to socialism need not require violent revolution.[1]

This colossal if muddled theory of history seemed intellectually impressive and was adopted by most European socialists during the late nineteenth century despite its overwhelming flaws. The labor theory of value was a fundamental fallacy. Nor did Marx's theory of history hold up under examination. Many major historical changes (e.g., the rise of Islam) cannot be correlated with changes in the means of production. "Primitive communism" probably never existed, although some civilized peoples, notably the Incas and the Javanese, practiced collective ownership of the means of production. Marx's political and economic predictions were not borne out. Marx had believed national differences would erode and be overtaken by growing class consciousness among the workers—at least within the Western context to which he believed his work applied. But nothing of the sort occurred. Nationalist sentiment remained far stronger than worker solidarity, as became apparent after the outbreak of World War I in 1914. The prophecy of progressive pauperization proved completely false; the industrial workers became better off, while the middle class increased in numbers. The concentration of wealth and class differences tended to decrease, not increase.

In the 1890s the flaws in Marxism had become apparent even to many socialists; a minority of right-wing socialists, the "revisionists," explicitly recognized this. Whether revisionist or not, most European socialists neither expected nor wanted violent revolution and were loyal supporters of the democratic form of government. There was little in that era to indicate that Marxism would lead to totalitarianism. The peculiar conditions in Russia and the genius of Lenin changed things.

Marxism was introduced into Russia in the 1880s. Ironically, while fanatically blocking the introduction of liberal democratic ideas, the tsarist censorship readily allowed the import of Marxist works as "scientific literature." Avoiding overtly revolutionary references, the literature of "legal Marxism" permeated the Russian intellectual scene long before Marxist parties were formed by some members of the Russian revolutionary movement. As a consequence, even the thinking of many nonsocialists in Russia was straitjacketed in Marxist categories.

A Russian Social Democratic Labor party was formed in 1898. (By contrast, the Russian liberal party, the Constitutional Democrats, or Cadets, for short, was organized only in 1905.) In 1903 the Social Democrats split, nominally over a question of organization, into two permanent factions, misleadingly called the Mensheviks, or "minority," and the Bolsheviks, or "majority," although the Mensheviks were actually the larger group until 1917. The Mensheviks tended to become an orthodox social democratic party not very different from similar parties in other European countries. Led by Lenin the Bolsheviks struck off in a different direction.

A Russian from the Volga region, Lenin belonged to the upper class. Trained as a lawyer, he became a revolutionary after his elder brother was executed for plotting to assassinate Tsar Alexander III. As a dogmatic Marxist he objected to any changes in the master's work other than the many unadmitted ones he was to introduce himself. He was an austere, energetic, and incredibly able political fanatic with a compelling need to dominate. Under a façade of democratic rhetoric, he was an elitist; in contradiction to the principal thrust of Marx's thought, he was a voluntarist who believed in the power of the will to overcome obstacles and "speed up" the course of history. Lenin brought an emphasis on the importance of *organization* to the revolutionary movement; not for nothing has his conception of the Communist party and its work been described as the development of "organizational weapons." And a striking aspect of Lenin's thinking, closely linked to his emphasis on organization, was his relentless militarism. Unlike most pre-1914 Marxists, Lenin often substituted the term "class war" for the conventional "class struggle." An admirer of Karl von Clausewitz, he once inverted the Prussian thinker's description of war and ironically described politics as "war carried on by other means." His writings even on peacetime matters are liberally sprinkled with terms of military origin such as "front," "cadre," and "vanguard."

Lenin's differences with the Mensheviks were at first vague, but a major conflict was his insistence on a narrow, conspiratorial party organization with a membership limited to active professional revolutionaries. This was arguably a necessity in the conditions existing in Russia in 1903, but Lenin insisted on this form of organization even after 1905 when a degree of liberty had been established. His attitude really stemmed from a deeper difference of views about humanity and the world. The Mensheviks and those socialists outside Russia who took an interest in the affairs of their Russian comrades jeered that Lenin's idea of the party resembled Louis XIV's idea of the state and that when Lenin spoke of the "dictatorship of the proletariat" (a phrase he invoked far more often than most Marxists), he really meant a "dictatorship *over* the proletariat." These diagnoses proved far more accurate than their authors realized. Lenin viewed a narrow, tightly controlled party as the "vanguard of the proletariat." Lenin maintained that left to themselves the workers would never become a revolutionary force. Their class consciousness would never develop beyond a drive for wage increases and reforms, and a properly organized party was necessary to lead them in the right direction. In Communist usage, "proletariat" often became merely a metaphor for the Communist party itself. In 1903 Lenin also invented a critical device by which the "vanguard party" could influence the masses—the distinction between the party's "minimum program" and "maximum program." While the latter expressed the ultimate aim of socialism, the minimum program expressed relatively short-term, reformist objectives, possibly even contradicting the maximum program, and was designed to win support from the masses of people outside the party.

Lenin analyzed the future of Russia in a way different from the Mensheviks. Both factions expected a "bourgeois-democratic revolution" in Russia that would end the tsarist autocracy. But the Mensheviks believed a considerable interval would lie between the "bourgeois-democratic revolution" and the eventual socialist revolution, for which Russia, a backward country, was far from ready. Marx, after all, had always envisaged the transition to socialism as beginning in the most advanced capitalist countries. However, Lenin, who detested "bourgeois" liberals far more than outright reactionaries, thought that the Russian bourgeoisie was weak. The proletariat must do much of its work even in the "bourgeois-democratic" phase and the revolution might be quickly transformed into a socialist one. Instead of emphasizing the alliance with the bourgeoisie as did the Mensheviks, the Bolsheviks envisaged an alliance between the working class and the peasantry. Lenin believed that despite Russia's backwardness, a socialist regime could be established and maintain itself provided socialist revolutions quickly followed in some of the more advanced Western countries. Revolution in Russia would hopefully trigger such revolutions. He borrowed this concept, confusingly designated "permanent revolution," from Leon Trotsky, who led a faction that cut a middle course between the Bolsheviks and the Mensheviks; it became a key to his thinking in 1917.

With the outbreak of World War I the world socialist movement suffered a dramatic split as socialists decided on their attitude toward the war. Most European social democrats backed their respective countries; but a minority, drawn from both the right and left wings of the prewar movements, opposed the war. Despite his extremism, Lenin had admired the leaders of the Socialist International, and especially the Germans; he now turned decisively against them. He took up a position of extreme opposition to the war, condemning all parties to it as "imperialist" and calling for "revolutionary defeatism." It was the obligation of all socialists in the belligerent countries to work against their own countries—but not out of pacifism. Lenin called for transforming "imperialist war" into civil war. Since few people felt that a series of civil struggles would be an improvement on the world war, this stand left the Russian Bolsheviks and a few groups from neutral countries isolated on the far left wing of the socialist movement. Lenin, never very popular with other socialists, was regarded as a half-mad crank.

Despite being ineffectual politically, Lenin embarked on the major theoretical study of his career, his work *Imperialism* (1916). Although not original (the work was largely derived from the writings of the British radical J. A. Hobson), it was to have an enormous impact far outside the ranks of the Communist movement. Lenin's theory of imperialism formed a major component not only of Communist doctrine but also of the "Third World" ideology that developed after World War II.

Imperialism performed a number of functions: It gave an explanation for World War I, explained away various gaps in Marxist doctrine that had become apparent over the last generation, and provided a basis for the development of the Communist movement in underdeveloped and colonial countries. Unlike most socialists of his era, Lenin had long been interested in developments in the colonial world. He suspected that they would play a larger role in world affairs than was generally believed.

Lenin explained that imperialism was not merely a political fact but the incurable last stage of capitalist development. It was a stage in which the domination of monopolies and financial institutions, rather than manufacturers, had been established and in which capitalism had to invest in the underdeveloped countries at the expense of the colonial peoples in order to maintain itself. Low costs for raw materials and labor in colonial areas produced "superprofits," some of which went to "bribe" part of the working class in the imperialist countries with higher wages. The resulting "workers' aristocracy" was the core of reformist socialism. This explained the "degeneration" (in Lenin's eyes) of the Socialist International and the failure of living standards to decline as Marx had predicted. Along with his theory of the need for a correctly organized vanguard, it also explained why there had been no revolution.

Unlike Hobson and earlier anti-imperialists, Lenin insisted that imperialism must continue until it was overthrown by force. The rival imperialist states not only would seize weak, underdeveloped countries but also would inevitably clash over their prey and would finally be driven to conquer each other. However, the resulting wars and the reactions imperialism produced in the colonial countries would generate revolutionary situations leading to the downfall of capitalism. Lenin accomplished an important shift in terminology and ideas by *identifying* capitalism and imperialism and not just postulating a causal link between the two. Like his theory as a whole, it was immensely influential among Asians and Africans who refused to accept Communist ideas in general against the West, and not only against those Western countries that had or once had had colonies. In Lenin's definition of imperialism, any country with external investments is "imperialist."[2]

To be sure, Lenin's theory was as remote from reality as it was influential. Imperialism did not explain either socialist reformism or workers' living standards. The Scandinavian socialists were reformists, although their nations had no colonies, while the French Socialists, whose country owned the second biggest colonial empire, were radically oriented; they were to become one of the few socialist parties to join the Communist International en masse. The living standards of the Scandinavian workers were far higher than those of the French and Belgian workers, despite the supposed existence of "superprofits" in the latter countries.

In fact, such "superprofits" did not exist, and investments in underdeveloped countries were peripheral to the economies of advanced lands. The developed countries mostly invested in and traded with each other, not with backward countries or colonies. There was little evidence that foreign investment injured the countries involved; Canada, for example, the largest single site of U.S. foreign investment, seems to have suffered little from the experience. The pattern of foreign investment bore little relation to that of imperial expansion in Asia and Africa. Over half of Britain's overseas investments went outside her empire entirely; in fact, the United States was the largest recipient of British capital. Most British investment within the empire went to the "white" empire of settler colonies like Canada and Australia, not to Asia and Africa. The fraction of British investment in the "nonwhite" empire went mostly to colonies such as India and Ceylon, where British rule was established long before the "imperialist" era of monopolies and finance capital, which Lenin dated to the last quarter of the nineteenth century. Less than a tenth of French investments went to French colonies, and the French empire as a whole was run at an economic loss. The U.S., German, Portuguese, and Italian empires were even less successful economically. Even those colonies that "paid" proved anything but indispensable. The Dutch, for example, whose home economy was more closely geared to their imperial possessions than the economy of any other Western nation, survived the loss of their empire in Indonesia and the subsequent complete confiscation of their investments without any trouble at all.

The rapid expansion of the Western colonial empires during the nineteenth century was due to a variety of causes, of which economic motives were by no means the most important. Sometimes Western traders or investors did secure the backing of their governments for their interests, but the dominant propelling force was political. The rivalries of the advanced Western countries were played out on a world stage as each power sought to match or block its rivals by snatching territory that *might* prove useful. Some colonies were seized for strategic reasons, especially by the British, who were content with the possessions they had gained in earlier eras of expansion but whose empire seemed to present many points of vulnerability to potential enemies. Disorders or misrule in areas adjacent to existing colonies tended to attract the extension of colonial rule as a "solution." Notions of military glory were still alive in Europe, and colonies were where glory could be won without much cost or many casualties. Even humanitarian motives—hatred of slavery, for example—played an important part, one probably more important in much of Africa than the search for profit. In any case, colonial expansion was peripheral to the mainstream of European international politics; the rivalries expressed in colonial expansion did not lead to a major war between the European great powers. In fact, such rivalries tended to cut across, rather than between, the alliance systems formed before World War I.[3] Indeed, World War I was caused not by overseas rivalries but by a crisis within Europe itself. Nor was this crisis related to the most mature "imperialist" powers' alleged need to subdue each other. The most advanced "capitalist" countries were the most reluctant to fight in 1914, as they were later most willing to give up their empires peacefully.

Its many errors notwithstanding, Lenin's theory of imperialism did become a landmark in world politics, and it showed its author's interest in international conflicts. Unlike many Western democrats, Lenin did not imagine he was living in a world that was about to become a peaceful place organized in a rational, democratic way under the rule of law. Lenin's attitude to war was, by his lights, coldly "realistic"; war would continue until capitalism had been abolished. Wars should be utilized, not stopped, and he welcomed the outbreak of war in 1914. In November 1914 he ridiculed the "pale and cowardly dream of unarmed struggle with the armed bourgeoisie, a sigh for the annihilation of capitalism without desperate civil war or a series of wars." There was no useful distinction between "aggressive" and "defensive" wars—at least in serious discussion as opposed to propaganda for the masses. The only proper distinction was between the class interests expressed by the war. Wars that furthered the revolution were good; those that hindered it were bad. He once commented that "we are struggling not against wars in general but against reactionary wars and for revolutionary wars."

Late in 1915 Lenin wrote "The United States of Europe Slogan," an article that pungently expressed his views. In a passage much admired and quoted by Josef Stalin, he explained that "unequal economic and political development is an indispensable law of capitalism. It follows that the victory of socialism is, at the beginning, possible in a few capitalist countries, or even in one taken separately. The victorious proletariat of that country, having expropriated the capitalists and organized socialist production, would stand up against the capitalist rest of the world, attracting to its cause the oppressed classes of other countries. It would stir up among them revolt among their capitalists, and if necessary, advance with military might against the exploiting classes and their states."

Shortly after, in "Some Theses," he outlined what he would do if the Bolsheviks came to power during the ongoing war: "We should propose peace to all the belligerents on condition of the liberation of colonies, and to all dependent and oppressed peoples not enjoying full rights. Neither Germany nor England nor France would under their present governments accept this condition. Then we should have to prepare and wage a revolutionary war, i.e., we should not only carry out in full by the most decisive measures our whole minimum program, but should systematically incite to insurrection all the peoples now oppressed by the Great Russians, all colonies and dependent countries of Asia (India, China, Persia, etc.) and also—and first of all—incite the proletariat of Europe to insurrection against its governments and in defiance of its social-chauvinists [i.e., patriotic socialists]. There is no doubt that the victory of the proletariat in Russia would create unusually favorable conditions for the development of revolution both in Asia and Europe." In 1916 Lenin's "Military Program of the Proletarian Revolution" remarked that "socialism victorious in one country does not exclude forthwith all wars in general. On the contrary, it presupposes them." While strongly implying in this document that wars would come primarily from the efforts of "bourgeois" countries to smash the socialist state or states, he also alluded to the duty to intervene in favor of the oppressed in "wars of liberation."[4]

After the Bolshevik seizure of power, Russia's relative weakness, the unexpected difficulty of organizing "socialist production," the fact that Lenin's expectations about the development of revolutionary situations in other countries proved exaggerated, all prevented the full and immediate implementation of this program. But, at least until 1956, the Soviet regime looked forward to future international wars, including a world war or a series of world wars, as part of the process of expansion of its form of socialism. It is important to note that the basic Communist policy on such matters was formulated before the Russian Revolution, and not, contrary to what some have claimed, only in response to the Allied intervention in the Russian Civil War.

Lenin's ideas, however, became of practical importance only thanks to events beyond his control. He spent most of his life from 1900 to 1917 in exile, and the Bolsheviks were not especially influential. They had played but a small role in the abortive revolution of 1905, and the more numerous Mensheviks had the allegiance of the organized elements of the Russian working class. Only the blunders of Russia's rulers and their democratic successors were to give Lenin's party the chance to seize power. Although the Bolshevik Revolution did not much resemble any later Communist victory, it and the events that followed it powerfully influenced the development of the Soviet regime and the Communist movement.

The Russian Empire and the Revolutions of 1917

In the early twentieth century Russia was a huge, multinational autocratic state. Climate, transportation difficulties, the tradition of despotism imposed by the Mongol conquerors, the persistence of serfdom, and the obscurantism of the state church had retarded Russia's development. But contrary to what is still widely imagined, Imperial Russia was not a primitive or static society; it was a country in the throes of rapid change.

The Russian Revolution, like the other revolutions in the modern world, followed a long period of rapid economic progress and occurred when that progress had been derailed and the deep fissures in Russian society opened under the stress of defeat in war. Although there was a surprising degree of social mobility in Russia, differences between social classes were sharp. The late development and restriction of political participation in Russia, the suppression of democratic forces, and the existence of an ignorant and land-hungry peasantry tended to promote extremism once the authority of the tsarist government disappeared.

Almost endless confusion has been caused by mistaken attempts to picture prerevolutionary Russia either as "advanced" like other continental European states or as "underdeveloped" like the countries of Africa, Asia, and Latin America. In fact, Russia occupied a position between the two extremes, though perhaps closer to that of the advanced industrial countries. Like Japan, Russia was a late-comer to the industrial world, still backward compared to Western Europe or North America but advanced compared to colonial Asia and Africa. Like Japan, which had begun its modernization at the same time in the 1860s, Russia was a complex society with relatively large cities, an advanced government administration, and an economic structure that was far more modern than those of most underdeveloped countries, even before modern industry was introduced. Unfortunately for Russia and the world, Russia's last tsars were not as capable as the Meiji emperor and his associates.

Despite poor leadership at the top, Russia was developing rapidly at the time of World War I. Although Russia's industrial development was uneven and still heavily dependent on imported foreign technology, she was overtaking France as the world's fourth industrial power. The country in general suffered from wildly uneven development: great modern factories loomed over fields tilled by a largely illiterate peasantry using methods outdated in Western Europe for centuries. Like their earlier counterparts in Western Europe, and perhaps inevitably, given their stage of development, Russian workers suffered from low living standards and poor working conditions—the average working day was ten hours. Most workers were little removed from the peasants, who had been serfs until 1861. Russian serfs had been chattel slaves with almost no rights, not serfs in the sense in which that term was understood in medieval Western Europe. The peasants believed that they had been cheated of their rightful share of the land after emancipation. Working inadequate dwarfholdings, they looked enviously at the estates of the nobility, who still owned a sixth of the land. Most Russian peasants still belonged to communes (*mir* or *obschina*) that parceled out land equally to their members, efficient or inefficient, in small, clumsily distributed strips. Until the abortive revolution of 1905 the Imperial government firmly upheld the authority of the communes while favoring the nobility at the expense of the peasants; thus Russia remained in fact and law an absolute monarchy in which all political activity was suppressed. Although Russia had some fine universities and produced scientists, engineers, and artists as good as any in the world, the last two tsars, Alexander III and Nicholas II (unlike their wiser Japanese counterparts), followed reactionary policies that actually opposed raising the educational level of the masses. Ruthless policies of anti-Semitism and of "Russification" of the non-Russian nationalities, who in fact formed a majority of the inhabitants of the empire, alienated much of the population. In these ways the Imperial government paved the way for its own downfall and the rise of communism.

The defeats inflicted by the Japanese during the Russo-Japanese War of 1904–05 and the resulting upheavals frightened even the nearly mindless Tsar Nicholas II, and he allowed the policies of the Russian government to take a sharp turn. Resentfully and reluctantly, a semiconstitutional regime was conceded. Political parties (including the Bolsheviks) were legalized, and a parliament, the Duma, although unrepresentative and with very limited powers, appeared. There was a quite remarkable freedom of speech and of the press. But the Duma was continually at war with the Imperial government, which clearly resented its existence, and the educated public remained generally hostile to the regime. The immense task of developing an effective system of popular education was begun. P. N. Stolypin, the empire's last great statesman, instituted a conservatively oriented land reform designed to free the peasants from the confines of the commune and form a class of efficient and contented small farmers. The "excess" peasants in overcrowded areas of European Russia would go to the cities to become workers or depart, with government help, for newly opened farmland in Siberia. The nobility was already gradually selling off its land to the more prosperous peasants and would be encouraged to continue doing so.

Had peacetime economic development and the reforms instituted after 1905 continued undisturbed for two decades, Russia might have peacefully become an industrialized constitutional monarchy.[1] As things were, however, less than a decade had elapsed when Russia stumbled into World War I under a weak, stupid ruler whom even monarchists despised. As W. H. Chamberlin, the greatest Western historian of the Russian Revolution, wrote, "When Nicholas II signed the order for the general mobilization of the Russian Army in 1914, he was unconsciously signing his own death warrant and that of the system which he embodied."[2]

The majority of Russians of all classes greeted the war with an outburst of patriotism, as did the peoples of the other warring countries. But the Russians suffered a series of appalling disasters that highlighted the imbecilities of their government. Although often successful against Austro-Hungarian and Turkish forces, the Russian armies suffered shattering defeats at the hands of the better-equipped and more efficient Germans. During 1915 there were not even enough rifles, and many Russian infantrymen entered battle unarmed until they picked up the weapons of men who had been hit. Although many of the worst shortages of equipment and supplies were relieved during 1916, and the Russians were able to launch a successful if very costly offensive, previous defeats, obvious incompetence at the top, and scandals in the court had destroyed much of what little respect the tsar and his government still commanded. Russia's now effective system of war production would make weapons for a very different conflict from that envisaged by its creators.

While elements of the upper class were contemplating a palace coup to replace the tsar, the Imperial government, hollowed out from within, collapsed with startling speed before a spontaneous popular uprising.[3] The downfall of the old regime was set off by a series of strikes and demonstrations in Petrograd. Food shortages—caused by the disorganization of the transportation system, and not by a poor harvest—crystallized general discontent. Troops sent to put down the demonstrators went over to their side instead. It became apparent that the monarchy had few supporters left. On March 15 the tsar abdicated, and no one in the line of succession would mount the throne. In the "February Revolution" (Russia was still on the Julian calendar, 13 days behind the modern Gregorian calendar), the old regime simply collapsed without much of a fight; there was little bloodshed at all outside the capital.[4]

The place of the old government was taken not by one regime but by two. A peculiar situation of "dual power" thus arose. The executive committee of the old Duma constituted a "Provisional Government," while even before this, on the initiative of moderate socialists, the workers and soldiers in Petrograd formed a "Soviet" (the Russian word for "council"). Similar Soviets arose all over the empire. Neither the Provisional Government nor the Soviets could claim to be truly representative bodies. The old Duma had been gerrymandered and elected on a very limited franchise, while the Soviets excluded the middle and upper classes and soldiers were heavily overrepresented at the expense of workers. The Soviets, however, were perceived as the more popular organs. At first they were dominated by the moderate socialist parties, the Mensheviks and the Socialist Revolutionaries. (The Socialist Revolutionaries were a non-Marxist group appealing primarily to the peasantry.) Following the doctrine laid down long before by the Socialist International, the socialist parties at first refused to take part in a "bourgeois" government, such as the Provisional Government was supposed to be. Thus the government was dominated by liberals; all the parties of the right had simply evaporated. The socialists did not consciously contest the authority of the government, but it soon became clear that in many ways the Soviets were the more powerful institution. The Soviet, not the government, really controlled the huge Petrograd garrison numbering over 160,000 men—if anybody did. Partly out of fear of a counterrevolution from the right, partly out of utopian notions about military affairs, and partly in response to pressure from below, the Petrograd Soviet issued an order explicitly extending a system of Soviets throughout the army and reducing what remained of the authority of the officer corps. In fact, a counterrevolution from the right was out of the question. The Provisional Government had already eliminated this possibility by promptly retiring 150 senior officers holding conservative beliefs. In April the Soviets developed an armed force of their own, the "Red Guards," a workers' militia.

Although led by men of good intentions, the Provisional Government was ineffective and remained so even when some of the moderate socialists overcame their scruples and turned it into a coalition government. The police, and to some extent the administration in general, had collapsed after the February Revolution. The liberals and moderate socialists were intent on prosecuting the world war, but they were unwilling to oppose the Soviets openly or try to restore discipline, something probably impossible in any case. The government took a legalistic attitude and insisted on waiting until a truly representative Constituent Assembly had been elected to undertake major reforms. Although all parties favored land reform and the government had seized the lands of the Church and the crown, it would not distribute them until the Constituent Assembly met. Unfortunately, elections for the assembly were delayed. Attempts to fill the gap with quasi-representative bodies—"democratic conferences" and a "Pre-Parliament"—proved ineffective.

The government was in an extremely difficult position. It was under terrific pressure from the Allies, who showed no comprehension at all of conditions in Russia. The Russian leaders genuinely believed in the war. Quite apart from any expansionist ambitions, all feared that a Russian withdrawal from the war would lead to a German victory. They were sure that a victorious Germany would subjugate Russia or restore the old regime. An early attempt to solve the land problem risked sparking desertions from the army as peasant soldiers sought to get home and make sure of their share of the land.

The government became increasingly out of touch with the lower classes. The February Revolution had been accompanied by a superficial upsurge of patriotism, but it soon became clear that the ordinary soldiers and the lower classes were fed up with the war. Even moderate socialists bitterly opposed the efforts of the liberals in the Provisional Government to maintain the annexationist aims of the old regime. And so patriotism, even in the most minimal sense, quickly died. One of the peculiarities of the Russian Revolution was the nearly nonexistent influence of nationalist sentiments among the Russians themselves (as opposed to the non-Russian nationalities). Instead, genuine internationalist sentiments were widespread. The revolution, in comparison with those of later decades, was marked by an unusual amount of idealism—although also by incredibly ferocious class hatreds.

The peasants, who developed their own system of land committees, began seizing estates. The movement of the peasants did not become really violent except in some of the "black-earth" provinces of south-central Russia, and the peasants were not interested in overthrowing the government. They knew and cared little about what went on in Petrograd and Moscow. But their actions showed the ineffectiveness of the government, which exercised little control outside the cities. And they further undermined the morale and discipline of the largely peasant army. The resulting situation was not created by the Bolsheviks, but they exploited it brilliantly.

Lenin had returned to Russia in April with German help. He plausibly explained away the assistance the Germans had provided to his return; unknown to all but a few Bolsheviks, he actually had a much more far-reaching relationship with the German government. The Germans had subsidized Lenin's party to a limited extent since the beginning of the war; they now greatly increased their financial help and ordered their own network of agents in Russia to assist Lenin's drive for power.

Lenin was disgusted to find that in the absence of his instructions a quite moderate attitude had been taken by the Bolsheviks, who were still small in numbers (they had under 10,000 members, although they had recently been gaining support among the Petrograd workers). Abandoning their antiwar stance, the leaders in Russia favored a "defensist" policy of supporting the new government. Lenin was convinced that a revolutionary situation was developing not just in Russia but in the rest of Europe. He hastily reversed the party's position, opposing the moderate socialists. He saw that the Soviets offered a road to power, that the Bolsheviks might gain a majority within the Soviets while playing them against the government. He expounded his policy in the "April Theses." "Revolutionary defeatism" still applied to the Provisional Government, which should be overthrown and replaced by a republic of Soviets committed to peace. The Bolsheviks adopted the land reform program of their Socialist Revolutionary rivals and demanded immediate implementation. The slogans of "Peace, Bread, and Land" and "All Power to the Soviets" expressed the party's new minimum program for appealing to the masses. Although the Bolsheviks were to make a number of tactical turns and suffer some ups and downs, the policy decided in April proved the key to victory. The Bolsheviks grew in strength and popularity, absorbing the *mezhrayontsy* group led by Trotsky, who became Lenin's chief lieutenant. Party membership grew to 240,000 by November 1917.

While Lenin tried to ride and steer the forces of disintegration, the Provisional Government committed fatal blunders. Given the state of the Russian army, the most that could reasonably have been expected of it was to hold its existing positions. But the generals and the government illogically decided that launching an offensive might restore the army's morale and cohesion. After scoring slight successes against Austro-Hungarian units, the attack turned into a disastrous rout and sparked demonstrations in the capital. Lenin did not feel ready to seize power, but the Bolsheviks let themselves be dragged into violent demonstrations by the Petrograd garrison. The Provisional Government managed to put down the demonstrations, and it cracked down on the Bolsheviks, driving the party temporarily underground and forcing Lenin to flee to Finland.

This reverse for Bolshevik influence was soon nullified, however. In August General Lavr Kornilov, the newly appointed commander-in-chief of the army, moved to reestablish discipline. Prime Minister Alexander Kerensky, a moderate socialist, was in at least partial agreement with Kornilov and authorized the dispatch of "reliable" forces to Petrograd. But Kerensky, perhaps because of blunders by go-betweens, then came to suspect— probably wrongly—that Kornilov planned to overthrow the government. (The full story of the "Kornilov affair" has never been fully disentangled.) To stop Kornilov's forces the panicky Kerensky called on all the forces of the left to help the government. In the face of such opposition, Kornilov's forces simply collapsed. The Bolsheviks regained their freedom of action and credit with the public, whereas the army command and the Constitutional

Democrats (who had been outspoken supporters of Kornilov) were discredited. They in turn hated Kerensky and were bitterly at odds with all except a few right-wing socialists. The socialists had also come to distrust Kerensky, who stayed in office only for lack of an obvious replacement. The gulf between liberals and socialists was a special feature of the Russian scene in 1917. It was typical of the socialists to arrogate the term "Russian democracy" to refer only to socialist groups, implying that nonsocialists were not democratic. To those involved the division between nonsocialist democrats and democratic socialists appeared as deep as that between the two groups and the Bolsheviks. While agrarian disorders continued, the government drifted on without a policy, except to wait for the Constituent Assembly, which was evidently expected to work miracles. The non-Bolshevik left focused its attention on the phantom of a new right-wing coup attempt.[5]

· An ideal situation had been created for the Bolsheviks, who quickly won over the support of most of the workers and critical elements of the army. The army was by this time nearly totally demoralized. There were enormous numbers of deserters, though most of the men were still willing to stay at the front if not asked to attack. Kornilov had hardly been beaten when the Bolsheviks gained a majority in the Petrograd Soviet: Trotsky became chairman of the Soviet on October 8. Shortly thereafter the Bolsheviks gained control of the Soviets of Moscow and the Urals, Volga, and Siberian regions. The Soviets were thus transformed into "front organizations" for the Bolsheviks, who could act in their name rather than that of their particular party—a major advance in dealing with the soldiers. Lenin was now sure that his party was strong enough to take power. For a time he pondered the possibility of a "peaceful transition," but by late September he settled on the need for an armed uprising. Many Bolsheviks were fearful of an open fight, and Lenin had to spend weeks in arguments, agitation, and bullying to secure the party's agreement to his policy. He sensed the need to beat the opening of the nationwide Congress of Soviets and the long-awaited elections for the Constituent Assembly, which would tend to stabilize the situation.

The Bolsheviks formed an informal alliance with the extreme left wing of the Socialist Revolutionaries and on October 12 secured the creation of the "Military Revolutionary Committee" by the Petrograd Soviet. This committee was used to issue orders to the garrison and conduct the uprising. Only in early November did Lenin finally overcome passive resistance within his own party to his plan, much of which—contrary to Communist myth—was hastily improvised at the last moment.

The Bolsheviks depended primarily on the pro-Bolshevik part of the Petrograd garrison, which was a minority of only 30,000–40,000 men; most of the troops were merely neutralized. The Red Guards or armed workers played only an auxiliary role; for the day of decision they assembled just 12,000 men out of hundreds of thousands of workers in Petrograd. The "October Revolution" was so far from being a "workers' uprising" that Lenin for a time seriously considered launching a purely military revolt outside Petrograd, using the firmly pro-Bolshevik Baltic Fleet and the Russian garrison in Finland to attack the city.

In early November an aura of menace overhung Petrograd, for a local German offensive had captured Riga and seemed to threaten the capital. Kerensky and his colleagues underestimated the Bolsheviks and wavered between complacency and apathy. The democratic socialists feared a Bolshevik coup mainly because they thought that it would merely pave the way for a right-wing take-over. There ensued a tug of war between the government commanders and the Military Revolutionary Committee for authority over the garrison. But the government failed to take resolute action and arrest the committee. As the Bolsheviks' final preparations became clear, the government took some countermeasures. The Petrograd garrison was ordered to stay in its barracks, and political commissars appointed by the Soviet were ordered removed. Units believed to be reliable were placed around the city to maintain checkpoints and guard key government institutions and public utilities. The government raised the drawbridges over the Neva River, the boundary between the working-class districts and the rest of the city. Late on November 6 Kerensky tried to close the

Bolshevik newspapers, while clashes took place at the draw-bridges.

Using these actions to claim that the government was menacing the Petrograd Soviet, the Bolsheviks covered their next moves with the claim that they were acting in self-defense. On the night of November 7 they went into action, aiming their attack primarily against communications and transportation centers, the Neva bridges, and the heart of the government. Neither side's soldiers were in a mood to shoot it out, and often the government's forces simply melted away. The only reserves at the government's disposal that had maintained their cohesion and were anti-Bolshevik were Cossacks; but they hated Kerensky for his "betrayal" of Kornilov, a fellow-Cossack, and demanded certain prerequisites and assurances before they would move. Kerensky gave the necessary promises, but his incompetent and irresolute garrison commander, Colonel Polkovnikov, failed to carry them out. (Kerensky bypassed or ignored the army chief of staff, General Alekseev, an able and intelligent man.) Within a few hours the authority of the government was restricted to its headquarters in the Winter Palace, which the Bolsheviks cautiously besieged. Contrary to legend, no dramatic "storming" of the palace took place. The revolutionary forces gradually infiltrated the sprawling building, and some of the defenders deserted. The morale of the remaining defenders crumbled after the Bolshevik cruiser *Aurora* arrived and opened fire. When the Bolsheviks announced their coup to the convening All-Russian Congress of Soviets, the democratic socialists angrily stalked out, leaving the Bolsheviks in control.

The coup had gone easily enough, yet the Bolshevik victory was far from complete. Convinced that the revolution was made, many pro-Bolshevik soldiers either deserted or went on an epic drunk to celebrate. Meanwhile the enemies of the new regime rallied. The Mensheviks encouraged a strike by government workers, and the Socialist Revolutionaries planned an uprising based on the Cossack and school units in Petrograd. Kerensky, who had escaped, failed to obtain troops from the nearby Northern Front—its troops were under heavy Bolshevik influence and the commanding general conceived his duty as holding the line against the Germans and remaining "neutral" in Russian politics. But the conservative Cossack general P. N. Krasnov, no friend of Kerensky, commanded a reserve cavalry corps near Petrograd. He collected a small force of 700 Cossacks, who were later joined by a similar number of cadets, and cautiously advanced toward the capital. Meanwhile the Bolsheviks had captured an officer carrying plans for the counter-uprising in Petrograd. Even so, the rebellion there on November 10 had some initial success, though the rebels were beaten in fighting far bloodier than that of November 7. Krasnov's uncoordinated attack reached Tsarskoe Selo amid large numbers of neutral troops. In a battle around Pulkovo on November 12, an immensely superior Bolshevik force of 8,000 men, built around a core of sailors from the Baltic Fleet, stopped Krasnov's force. The sailors managed to outflank the anti-Bolsheviks, who were already worried about the neutral forces behind them. Krasnov's men could expect little help, for the Menshevik-dominated railroad workers union had decided to "prevent civil war" by refusing to transport troops anywhere; this worked in favor of the Bolsheviks. His men demoralized, Krasnov retreated and was forced to call for an armistice. The Bolsheviks professed to be ready to compromise if Kerensky was handed over to them, and the Cossacks agreed. Kerensky barely managed to escape; this was the end of serious resistance in the north.

The Bolsheviks had to fight a major battle for Moscow, whose government was dominated by men far more resolute than Kerensky. The center of Russian business enterprise and of liberalism, Moscow was politically more moderate than Petrograd. Even the local Bolsheviks were reluctant to fight, and they went into action only after the fall of the Winter Palace. The troops loyal to the hastily organized local Military Revolutionary Committee held the Kremlin and took control of the heavy artillery in the Moscow area. But the progovernment forces boldly attacked and seized the Kremlin on November 10. Bitter street fighting broke out. On November 12 Mensheviks and Left Socialist Revolutionaries arranged an armistice; like so many future truces between Communists and their enemies, this worked in favor of the Bolshevik forces. The Bolsheviks regrouped and brought up reinforcements, whereas their opponents were demoralized by the news of Krasnov's defeat in the north. When the armistice expired, the Bolsheviks recaptured the Kremlin. On November 15 the government forces surrendered. Most of the rest of Russia followed the lead of the capitals, and the Bolsheviks soon overcame the desultory resistance of the army headquarters at Mogilev.[6]

The new regime's power was shaky in the areas of Russian empire inhabited by non-Europeans. The latter, like the Russian peasantry, had temporarily been neutralized by Bolshevik promises. Against his basic inclination toward centralism and against the wishes of most Bolsheviks, Lenin had "adopted" the Socialist Revolutionary program for a federal Russian empire, to which he added demagogic promises of "self-determination." The new regime did not control the Cossack areas in southern Russia, and the Bolsheviks' attempt to take power in the Ukraine misfired. There the Ukrainian nationalist Rada ("council," a Ukrainian synonym for "Soviet") had allied itself with the Bolshevik-dominated Kiev Soviet to chase out the Provisional Government. The Rada then fell out with the Bolsheviks and seized power in Kiev for itself, proclaiming a Ukrainian People's Republic on December 3. It did not, however, have effective control of the whole of the Ukraine; the Soviet at Kharkov in the east held out.[7]

It has often been said that given the trend of left extremism in Russia in 1917, the Bolsheviks' seizure of power was no great achievement; indeed, their real feat was to stay in power. Only the latter part of this common view is justified, however. Only Lenin's energetic leadership got the Bolshevik takeover going; had further delays occurred, the party might have forfeited the chance to seize power. Yet Lenin was an outlaw for much of 1917 and was lucky to avoid arrest. At any number of points the Bolshevik drive for power could have been derailed. The case of Romania, with a society similar in many ways to Imperial Russia and a government even more incompetent and oppressive, shows that the problems of Russia, although fearsome, were not insoluble. After Romania irresponsibly blundered into World War I in 1916, its army practically disintegrated under the impact of an Austro-German counteroffensive. The rulers of Romania, a group not usually noted for statesmanship, then hastily arranged a general land reform. After losing half the country without much of a fight, the Romanian peasant soldiers responded with patriotic fervor. The army was reorganized with the help of a French military mission and stood fast in the defense of the rest of Romania. Although mixed with demoralized Russian units, the Romanians retained their cohesion and surrendered only after Russia's collapse left them isolated. Romania remained completely resistant to Communist influence and proved a bulwark against the spread of communism in 1919–20.

The overwhelming faults of the Provisional Government were its failures to see that the army could no longer carry on the war and that nothing could stop the peasants' seizure of the land, an effort which the parties comprising the government did not actually oppose in principle. Without the peace and land issues Lenin would have had nothing on which to build a base of support. Perhaps less easy to explain is the Russian socialists' easygoing attitude toward their Bolshevik rivals. Most of the Mensheviks and the Socialist Revolutionaries remained startlingly blind to the real aims and motives of Lenin, a man they knew well and disliked.

Even within its self-imposed prison of legalism and "war to the victorious end," the Provisional Government still had a number of opportunities to save itself. Although the huge Petrograd garrison violently refused to go to the front, it might have been safely demobilized or dispersed into the interior. The government might also have moved at an early date to the much more favorable political climate of Moscow, as it belatedly decided to do on October 18. Had Kerensky chosen and relied on better military subordinates, the countermeasures belatedly ordered to meet the Bolshevik threat might have been better carried out and the Cossacks rallied to the regime.

The victorious Bolsheviks hastily announced the creation of a republic based on the Soviets and decreed that the land was to pass into the hands of the peasants. The Bolsheviks embarked on a number of sensible reforms of the calendar and alphabet. They also began to nationalize industry and large properties and to take over effective control of the government administration. Both tasks proved far more complex and difficult than Lenin had expected.

Over the objections of many Bolsheviks Lenin rejected proposals for a compromise with the Mensheviks and the Socialist Revolutionaries and for a socialist coalition government. The Bolsheviks would rule as the overwhelmingly dominant force, and as a dictatorship. They were, however, not yet strong enough to prevent or seriously interfere with the long-planned elections for the Constituent Assembly on November 25. The election showed that the Socialist Revolutionaries had overwhelming popular support. The Bolsheviks received only 24 percent of the vote, and their Left Socialist Revolutionary allies got just 5 percent. Lenin pondered the problem of how to dispose of the embarrassment of the assembly while he reinforced his dictatorship. On December 11 the Constitutional Democrats were outlawed; on December 20 the Cheka, or secret police, perhaps the most characteristic feature of the Communist state, was founded. On December 22 Lenin reformed his regime as a coalition; the Left Socialist Revolutionaries, a rather confused and flighty group, took over some positions in the government. The Bolsheviks then proceeded to tackle their socialist enemies. On December 30 a number of leaders of the right wing of the Socialist Revolutionary party were arrested. When the Constituent Assembly bravely met in January 1918, it was dispersed by force.

In external affairs the new government undertook dramatic moves. On November 8 the Bolshevik rump of the Congress of Soviets issued a "Decree on Peace," couched in Wilsonian rather than Leninist terminology, appealing to the belligerents to make peace. As Lenin had expected, it was ignored. He went on to arrange armistice talks with the Central Powers, which opened on December 15. Openly revolutionary propaganda was launched against both the Central Powers and the Allies, but perhaps emphasizing the latter. On December 3 the Soviet government issued a "Declaration to all Moslem Toilers of Russia and the East." It promised religious and other freedoms to Moslems within the former Russian empire and urged the Moslem subjects of other empires, and especially those of India (which had recently been promised self-government by Britain) to revolt against their ruler. On December 24 the Soviet government announced that it had appropriated 2 million rubles for the "left internationalist wing of the labour movement of all countries."[8]

The Western democracies viewed the new regime with disgust and refused to recognize it. At bottom, however, they did not regard it as very important in itself, much less as a major threat. They were absorbed in the war with Germany. Further, although angry at the Bolsheviks, British foreign secretary Balfour set the tone of their policies when he remarked that it was not in Britain's interest to have an "open breach with this crazy system." The Western powers no more understood the Bolsheviks than they feared them. It was widely believed that the Bolsheviks were merely the agents of Imperial Germany and/or a Jewish conspiracy. In an even stranger misunderstanding, they were often described as "anarchists." It was commonly believed both on the left and right that the Bolshevik government actually represented the rule of the lower classes, although most of its leaders were actually of middle- or upper-class origin. On both sides of the battle fronts of the world war and in Russia itself, it was generally believed that the new regime would not last very long.[9]

For the next two years its existence did hang by a thread on a number of occasions. Circumstances were to lead, against the will of both sides, to the first armed clash between the Western democracies and a Communist regime.

Civil War and Intervention

The Russian Civil War began as a comparatively small-scale effort by the Bolsheviks to subdue the Don, Kuban, and Ural Cossacks, who had refused to recognize their authority, and to conquer the Ukraine from the nationalist Rada. This small struggle was to grow into a great struggle of incredible ferocity, plunging Russia in a "nightmare of unparalleled suffering." War, massacre, famine, and epidemics were to result in 9 million deaths. Militarily, it was a war of spectacular movement by small armies and bizarre technological contrasts; tanks and planes played a major role, yet it was the last war in which horse cavalry operated on a large scale.

The Don and Kuban Cossacks became the hard core of the resistance to the Soviet regime in European Russia. The Cossacks were a peculiar group, descended from highly militarized frontiersmen who had fled serfdom to colonize the southern steppes. Their ancestors had finally submitted to the Imperial government but had retained a degree of self-rule in return for rendering military service at their own expense. The Cossacks were prosperous farmers by Russian standards and far better educated than most of the peasantry. But they shared their lands with other groups. Although the Cossacks formed a majority of the rural population in the Don and Kuban provinces, a majority of the population as a whole were non-Cossack tenant farmers or industrial workers, loosely called *inogorodny* (literally, "people from other towns"). Although the non-Cossack farmers were well-off by Russian standards, they were much poorer as a group than the Cossacks, and they lacked political rights. In 1917 the Cossacks had been relatively unaffected by the revolutionary upsurge. As their newly elected Ataman (governor), General Kaledin, drily remarked, never having been serfs, they were not intoxicated by freedom. But they were bitterly at odds with the jealous *inogorodny.*

The Don offered the best, perhaps the only, haven for the Whites, as the resistance to the Bolsheviks was now called. After the October Revolution, Generals Kornilov, Alekseev, and others fled there. Kaledin let them organize an all-Russian anti-Bolshevik force, the Volunteer Army. It consisted mainly of officers from the old army, now in the process of complete dissolution. Although many officers were undoubtedly monarchists, the leaders of the army were not reactionaries; they accepted the February Revolution. (It is interesting to note that most of the White leaders came from "lower" social origins than most of their Bolshevik counterparts.) Unfortunately, the Whites were never able to agree on their positive political aims.

The Volunteers helped Kaledin defeat an attempted Bolshevik coup in December 1917. Although the Bolsheviks did not have much positive support, Kaledin found that his own position was weak. The return of Cossack units from the disintegrating front should have given him a huge armed force, but the young Cossack veterans were in no mood to fight anyone and had been influenced by the general atmosphere of demoralization.

Having failed to conquer the Ukraine and Don from within, the Bolsheviks prepared to subdue them from without. The Ukrainians refused an ultimatum demanding that they cooperate with the Bolsheviks against Kaledin and stop disarming Soviet units in their territory. Assembling a force of pro-Bolshevik army units and Red Guards, the Red commander, Antonov-Ovseenko, launched a double drive against the Rada and the Don. The Rada's forces were low in morale, and the Red forces soon overwhelmed them, taking Kiev on February 8, 1918. However, the Bolsheviks had little popular support in the Ukraine and failed to make their rule effective. While the Ukrainian party leaders quarreled among themselves, the ill-disciplined Red troops ran wild.

Although Cossacks proved tougher opponents, they were out-flanked by the conquest of the Ukraine and politically divided. General Kaledin was a conservative in all-Russian matters but a liberal reformer at home. He insisted that the restive *inogorodny* be brought into the government. The *inogorodny* were at least equivocal toward the Bolsheviks, and the Cossacks' own morale was shaky. The attempt to reform the Don government in the midst of a war was not successful. There were several hard-fought battles, but some Cossacks went over to the Red side, and in February 1918 Cossack resistance began to collapse. Kaledin shot himself in despair and in March the Red Forces overran the Don. Gross blunders by the Red command allowed some of their most determined foes to escape. A force of 1,500 Cossacks fled to the Salsk steppe, while the Volunteer Army, numbering 4,000 men, marched south to the Kuban Cossack territory—only to find that it was under Red control. It seemed for a time as though the Civil War was almost over. Indeed, if not for some blunders by the Bolshevik leaders, it might have been.[1]

The peace talks between the Bolsheviks and the Central Powers at Brest-Litovsk saw a curious situation, and the first Communist attempts at diplomacy. Although the Soviet regime was nearly helpless militarily and was subsidized by Germany—a fact known only to Lenin and his closest colleagues—the Bolsheviks resolved to play for time. They hoped to use the peace talks as a forum for revolutionary propaganda and as a means of "exposing" the real aims of the Central Powers and the Allies. Several times they tried to move the negotiations to Stockholm, where the chances for publicity were better. They hoped that even if revolution did not immediately result, internal disturbances would at least weaken the Central Powers and force them to grant better terms to the Soviet regime.

The Central Powers in their turn wanted peace badly so that they could concentrate their forces in the West and draw desperately needed food supplies from the Ukraine. At first their diplomats were conciliatory; they wished to end military operations in the east and avoid being put at a disadvantage in the propaganda war. Lengthy debates ensued during which both sides mouthed "democratic" formulas of a peace without annexations and indemnities and belched slogans about self-determination. The Central Powers demanded "self-determination" for Poland, Lithuania, and the part of Latvia under their control, meaning the maintenance of their puppet regimes there; whereas the Soviets insisted that the real will of the people involved could be ascertained only if the Germans and Austrians left. Trotsky, the chief Soviet negotiator, played a skillful game, and there were strikes and immense peace demonstrations in Germany and Austria-Hungary. But the governments of those states stood firm. Fed up, they opened contact with the Rada, which had previously been pro-Allied. The Bolsheviks were handed a quasi-ultimatum, while the Central Powers signed a treaty with the Rada.

Most Bolsheviks were horrified at the idea of accepting "imperialist" terms and preferred to launch a "revolutionary war." Lenin sensibly pointed out that revolution in the west was not imminent and under the circumstances war meant suicide. Trotsky proposed an intermediate stance of returning to Brest-Litovsk with the formula "no war, no peace," refusing to sign a peace treaty and in effect daring the Germans to attack a passive opponent and risk an eruption behind their lines. Against Lenin's will he was authorized to go ahead.

The Central Powers were less than overwhelmed; they decided to occupy the whole of the Baltic States and the Ukraine.

Their advance met little resistance, and the Soviets had to submit to new and far harsher terms, obliging them to evacuate the Ukraine and Finland, where a local civil war was raging between Whites and Reds. Central Powers and Rada troops overran the Ukraine, where they were met with relief if not enthusiasm, and the Germans sent a small expeditionary force to support the Finnish Whites. During March 1918, not certain where the Germans would stop, the Bolsheviks hastily transferred their government to Moscow to get farther away from them. In the same month they renamed their party "Communist."

The Bolsheviks' foolish attempt to play for time had probably cost them both the Ukraine and Finland, for the Central Powers had originally accepted them as the rulers of the whole Russian empire. Only their delaying tactics had caused the Central Powers to improvise a separate peace with the Ukraine.[2]

The German advance deprived the Soviets of much of their food supply and industry and helped to revive the Civil War. In order to cover the eastern border of the Ukraine, the Germans decided to make a limited advance into the Don Cossack territory. Soviet control had never been firmly established there outside the big towns, and a mere month of Soviet misrule drove the infuriated Cossacks to revolt in April 1918. The few local Communists had been shoved aside by outsiders who knew little about the area. Hasty nationalization, forced requisitions of food, political persecution and outrages committed by the badly disciplined occupation forces and Red Guards fleeing from the Ukraine, all had enraged the population. Soon the Reds held only a few cities and the main rail lines; the arrival of the Germans in May finished off Soviet rule in the Don. General Krasnov, now professing friendship for Germany, was elected Ataman and with German aid created a well-equipped army numbering 60,000 men.

The Volunteer Army had been repulsed in its attempt to liberate the Kuban. It now returned to the Don somewhat stronger in numbers, having absorbed many Kuban Cossack volunteers. There it obtained a badly needed period of rest. Meanwhile General Anton I. Denikin had become the effective commander of the Volunteer Army because Kornilov had been killed and Alekseev was deathly ill. Krasnov now urged Denikin to join him in an offensive to liberate the northern part of the Don territory and capture Tsaritsyn (later renamed Stalingrad, and still later, Volgagrad). Tsaritsyn was an industrial and transportation center on the Volga whose retention was vital if the Soviets were to keep grain and fuel moving from the Caucasus to central Russia. As Krasnov and many later critics observed, the Soviet forces in the

North Caucasus were numerous but badly organized and would have withered away had a White victory on the Volga isolated them. But though in many ways the ablest of the White leaders, Denikin refused this apparently sensible proposal. He and many of his men conceived of the Volunteer Army as an anti-German resistance force as well as an anti-Bolshevik organization. They could not stomach the idea of close cooperation with the Germans, although they were reluctantly willing to accept from Krasnov arms that had originally been provided by Germany. Perhaps more important, the many Kuban Cossacks in their ranks demanded the liberation of their homeland, and Denikin must have feared mutiny if their wishes were not respected. The Volunteer Army thus marched south, in the wrong direction from the point of view of grand strategy, splitting the anti-Communist war effort. Nevertheless, both the Volunteers and the Don Army scored tremendous successes. Krasnov marched on Tsaritsyn while Denikin liberated the Kuban and went on to clear the rest of the North Caucasus. The Soviet regime was now threatened by a major war front in the south just as another blunder in policy opened a front in the east and provoked Allied intervention.[3]

Since late 1917 the Western powers had indecisively tried to back various opponents of the Bolsheviks, notably Ataman Kaledin and the Rada, in the hope that an eastern front against Germany could be reconstituted. They had also briefly negotiated with the Bolsheviks themselves when in later February and early March the latter feared that the Germans would overthrow them. In practice, however, the Allies did not do very much. The British and French would have been happy to see a large Japanese force land in Siberia and march west, with or without Soviet approval. But the Japanese were reluctant to move alone, and the Americans rightly thought that a Japanese force in Siberia would neither move far enough west to engage the Germans nor leave when the war ended.

An Allied force was already stationed in Russia. This was the 50,000–man Czechoslovak Corps, which had been formed largely out of Czech soldiers who had defected from the Austro-Hungarian army. The Czechs had not interfered in Russian politics; they had fought side by side with the Reds against the Germans in the Ukraine. For a time the Czechs were stationed close to Moscow, and they could easily have overthrown the Soviet government had they so desired. British and French planners briefly considered using the corps against the Soviets in order to recreate an eastern front. But the Czechs wanted to get out of Russia, and the French, their chief friends in the Western alliance, wanted them on the western front. It was decided to remove the Czechs from Russia via the Trans-Siberian railroad and the port of Vladivostok. The Soviets agreed.

In May 1918 the Czech Corps, partly disarmed, was strung out over a distance of thousands of miles along the Trans-Siberian railroad. Ugly incidents between the Czechs and Central Powers prisoners of war sparked the suspicions of the Communists; some of the Czech officers were anticommunist Russians, and the Czechs were carrying more weapons than allowed in their agreement with the Soviets. On May 23 Trotsky, now the Soviet commissar for war, ordered the Czechs disarmed and interned. This proved a disastrous mistake, for the Czechs were far stronger and better organized than the Soviet forces in Siberia. They resisted attack easily, and with the help of anticommunist Russians they quickly gained control of the whole area between the Volga and the Pacific. Turning west, they and their allies marched toward Moscow.

The Czech revolt and other pressures outside Russia finally provoked the Western powers to intervene. The British and French saw the Czech revolt as a chance to revive the eastern front, and the Americans changed their minds. President Wilson feared that the Czechs were greatly outnumbered, and it was believed that many of the troops fighting them were really armed German and Austrian prisoners—wild rumors of a takeover of Siberia by armed enemy prisoners had been circulating for months. Rescuing an Allied force under attack, as opposed to a major intervention designed to pursue the misty vision of a restored eastern front, seemed a worthy objective to Wilson. Since the Japanese could not be trusted to intervene alone, Wilson decided on July 4 to send a U.S. force to Siberia. Wilson made clear his plan to send a limited force of 7,000 Americans and a comparable number of Japanese to guard the Czech lines of communications. He specifically rejected the reestablishment of an eastern front and by implication dismissed any aim of overthrowing the Communist regime.

Two U.S. regiments quickly reached Vladivostok. They and the Japanese, who sent in a force ten times the size of the U.S. contingent, arrived to find that the Czechs already had the situation well in hand. As Wilson had expected, the Japanese refused to move west of Lake Baikal. The Japanese and Americans settled down to watch each other, thousands of miles east of the true front line, playing no real role in the Civil War.

However, the Japanese behaved as brutally then as they would later in World War II. They subsidized a number of semibandit Siberian Cossack leaders who were only nominally subordinate to the White headquarters in western Siberia. The Japanese and their local allies soon enraged the originally apathetic Siberian peasants into waging a guerrilla war against them, seriously interfering with the working of the Trans-Siberian railroad, the main supply line of the Whites. The East Siberian guerrillas fought one or two skirmishes with the Americans but soon realized they had no quarrel with them. They reached an informal truce with the Americans and left the sector of the Trans-Siberian guarded by the Americans alone. The overall effect of the Siberian intervention was to injure the Whites seriously by disrupting their rear. The presence of the U. S. forces did help to preserve Russia's territorial integrity by inhibiting the Japanese. But it is doubtful whether the Japanese seriously intended to obtain permanent control over Siberia.

North Russia was the only other theater of the Russian Civil War where major Allied forces appeared. As in World War II the Western powers had shipped large quantities of war supplies by the northern sea route to Archangel and Murmansk. The inadequate railroad system caused large amounts of supplies to pile up at the ports. When Russia left the war, the Allies wished to repossess the supplies, or at least keep them from falling into German hands.

Thus arrival of a German force in Finland in March 1918 seemed to pose a serious threat. The Allies feared the Germans might capture the supplies and establish submarine bases there, enabling the U-boats to bypass the mine barriers the Allies were establishing to seal off the passages to the North Sea. (Actually, the Germans had no such intentions.) Loosely interpreting a permissive message sent by Trotsky at a difficult moment during the Brest-Litovsk talks in March 1918, the local authorities at Murmansk allowed a British naval squadron long-stationed at Murmansk to disembark marines. Ironically, the small British force clashed with some White Finns who were pursuing their Red Finn enemies into Russian territory. The British stayed ashore at Murmansk despite Moscow's disapproval. They and the French wished to send forces to Archangel when the White Sea ice broke up. Short of troops, they badgered the Americans to supply a force. On July 17 President Wilson reluctantly agreed to provide a single regiment to guard war stores in northern Russia. With the Czech-Soviet struggle well underway, no one showed much interest in Soviet objections.

On August 2 a small British and French force, with the help of an anticommunist uprising, occupied Archangel. When the Americans arrived, they were placed under British command, although they formed a majority of the Allied troops in the area. The British decided to embark on a far more aggressive campaign than Wilson had envisaged. Pushing up the Dvina River and the Archangel-Vologda railroad, they penetrated far inland. During 1918–19 there was periodically heavy fighting on the North Russian front. But the Allies were unable to form an effective White Russian force, and their own forces were very limited—there were probably never more than 25,000 Allied and White troops in the area. Distance, poor communications, and difficult terrain prevented the area from becoming a decisive theater of war. The U.S. forces were withdrawn in the spring of 1919, the earliest time after the end of World War I that their safe evacuation was possible. North Russia was the only theater of the Russian Civil War where the Allies, rather than the White Russians, were the primary force on the anti-communist side.[4] A tremendous amount has been written about the Allies' intervention in the Russian Civil War, yet the Allies did not in fact play a decisive role in the struggle. The actions of the Germans had a far greater impact; their policies were complex, even bizarre, involving them simultaneously in financial support to Lenin, military occupation of much of Russia, and aid to the Don Cossacks.

The Soviets were rather lucky to excape being crushed between the Allies and the Germans. The latter seriously reconsidered their relations with the Bolsheviks in the summer of 1918. The saner elements in the German government were beginning to suspect that a horrible mistake had been made in helping the Bolsheviks. Both liberals and principled conservatives felt moral qualms about the relationship with the Communist regime; even Ludendorff and the Kaiser's court recognized that there was something horrible and absurd about a conservative monarchy propping up regicidal revolutionary fanatics. The twists and contradictions in Germany's Russian policy were about to be ironed out in favor of an all-out war against the Soviets. However, a series of defeats on the western front in July-August 1918 made it clear that Germany could just not afford a new front in the east. Instead, the increasingly desperate Germans drew closer to the Soviets and considered plans for a joint campaign against the Allied beachhead in North Russia and the White forces in the south. But further defeats in the West prevented the execution of such plans, probably fortunately for the Soviets. Even had they been successful, perhaps especially had they been successful, they might well have fatally entangled the Soviet cause with that of the doomed German empire.[5]

Only tremendous exertions and feats of organization enabled the new Soviet state to survive. It hastily created new armed forces and a regimented economy to supply them. Like their White enemies, the Communists quickly learned that nothing could be done with the remnants of the old army; a new one had to be built up. Consequently, a new Red Army was announced in February 1918. Despite his blunders at Brest-Litovsk and in dealing with the Czechs, Trotsky proved one of the great war ministers of history. The Soviet regime was at first too weak to enforce conscription; thus the Red Army was developed about a core of volunteers drawn mostly from the working class. It was clear after the Czech revolt, however, that more men were needed, and so a draft was introduced. "Bourgeois" men were restricted to noncombat duties. Over much opposition Trotsky enforced the use of "specialists"—officers of the old army of middle- or upper-class origin who acted as advisers and then became commanders in the field. They were carefully controlled by political commissars and a system that held their families hostage. The result was the formation of an army of 800,000 men by 1919, and of 3 million men a year later. Traveling in a specially equipped armored train, Trotsky frequently visited the fighting fronts at critical moments to supervise the local commanders.

During the first half of 1918 the Communist party had solidified its control, ejecting Mensheviks and Right Socialist Revolutionaries from the local Soviets and cracking down on political opposition. The Soviets and the Unions were transformed from popular institutions to instruments of party control. The workers' attempts to run industry themselves—an effort stigmatized by Communists as "anarchosyndicalism"—were curbed, and the working class was in effect broken to harness by the totalitarian state in which it supposedly exercised a "dictatorship." Lenin himself admitted that a majority of the workers came to support the Mensheviks during 1918.

The Left Socialist Revolutionaries had opposed the Brest-Litovsk peace and were increasingly at odds with the Bolsheviks; they tried to overthrow the Soviet government in July 1918 but were promptly crushed. This episode and the intensification of the Civil War led to an outright policy of terror in which all possible enemies of the regime were hunted down. This "Red Terror" cost an estimated 140,000 lives. An equal number of people are estimated to have been killed in the process of crushing the peasant insurrections that became a common occurrence in 1918. The peasant uprisings were generally not "political" in nature. They were caused by the economic policies of the regime.

Circumstances caused Lenin to force the pace of nationalization rather more quickly than he would have liked, and this aspect of the Communist program was implemented much faster in Russia than in any later Communist country. Fears of the consequences of leaving any important enterprises under private control during the Civil War, interacting with ideological suppositions about "socialism," caused the institution of a regime of drastic nationalization and ultra-centralized control over the economy. This policy of "War Communism" substituted bureaucratic control for even the most piddling transactions. The Communists did not understand the importance of trade or money, and they tended to suppose that running the economy was simply a matter of directing what was going on in the factories. In fact they merely created a strangling bureaucracy for which they did not have sufficient personnel. The normal give and take between town and country broke down. Peasants were planting less and did not ship food to the cities, which were producing insufficient goods to pay for food. The currency was by this time worthless. The Communists "solved" the problem by trying to exercise control over the countryside by playing the poorest peasants against the rest and by requisitioning at gunpoint. The results of this policy were a series of bloody insurrections. Probably the Soviets would have been wiser to institute the policies later put into operation in 1921: stopping and reversing nationalization and instituting a small tax in kind on peasant households to obtain grain.

War Communism and the Soviets' food policies were not a success in economic terms. Both industrial and agricultural production continued to decline until 1921. Nonetheless the Soviet government did produce enough war material to supply its army, and during 1918 it managed to break the resistance of the peasantry in the central provinces of Great Russia, ensuring a stable rear by the time of the decisive battles of the Civil War in 1919.[6] Despite doctrinaire economic policies, Lenin exercised his usual tactical flexibility in dealing with political questions. Having broken any overt opposition, Lenin decided in late 1918 to "manage" discontent and win over undecided elements by tolerating the "Legal Opposition." This consisted of those Mensheviks and Right Socialist Revolutionaries who opposed any armed struggle against the Bolsheviks; they were allowed a very limited degree of freedom.[7]

Political cleverness, utter ruthlessness, and organizational feats outweighed the economic weakness of the Communist regime and enabled it to hold off its enemies. The Czechs and their Russian allies managed to capture Kazan, but in September 1918 their march to the west was stopped at Sviazhsk. There a force of 3,000–4,000 Red Army troops managed to throw back 2,000 Whites. This tiny battle proved a turning point. Tediously bringing small warships from the Baltic by river and canal, the Reds assembled a flotilla on the Volga. They retook Kazan and soon drove the Whites back to the Ural Mountains, recapturing vital supplies of grain and reopening the Volga as a supply line. The Siberian White forces were torn by political quarrels and soon lost their effectiveness. The old division between socialists on the one hand and liberals and officers on the other revived. On November 18 a military coup supported by the Cadets overthrew the Siberian government and installed Admiral Alexander Kolchak as "temporary" military dictator. The coup alienated the Socialist Revolutionaries and their Czech allies. The latter, in any case, were losing any enthusiasm for fighting with the end of World War I.

In the south a seesaw struggle raged in the steppes around Tsaritsyn until early 1919. The Reds managed to form a coherent southern front and stopped repeated attacks by the Don Cossacks. In the same period the Volunteer Army, fighting immensely superior numbers of badly organized and led Red Army troops, managed to conquer the whole of the North Caucasus. The remnants of the Soviet forces finally had to flee across the desert to the lower Volga in a horrifyingly costly death march. Denikin had secured the White rear to the south and was free just in time to turn his forces north.

With the end of the world war the Germans abandoned the Ukraine. "Hetman" Pavlo Skoropadsky's conservative puppet regime, which the Germans had substituted for the Rada when the latter had failed to deliver the grain they had demanded, tried to hang on. The Ukrainian nationalist Directory, which had succeeded the Rada, formed an alliance with the Soviets against Skoropadsky. When Skoropadsky was disposed of, the Red Army predictably turned on the nationalists and recaptured Kiev. Neither the nationalists nor the Reds could form an effective government in the Ukraine. The countryside was reduced to a state of complete chaos, dominated by bands of peasant guerrillas, some loyal to the Reds, some loyal to Ukrainian nationalism, and some loyal to anarchist ideals. Most, however, seemed interested primarily in looting, or massacring Jews, 50,000 of whom were killed during 1919.

Despite their inability to control the Ukraine effectively, the Soviet forces threatened the western flank of the Don Cossacks. The latter were becoming demoralized, and early in 1919 the Red Army finally forced them back, overrunning much of the northern Don. Denikin's forces arrived from the south just in time to prevent a complete collapse in the Don area.[8]

With the end of the world war disappeared the original impetus for the Allied intervention in Russia. The Allied leaders had to decide a fundamental policy toward the Soviet government. Only now did the question of relations with the Soviet regime become the primary determinant of the Western powers' policy in Russia; until November 1918 the war with Germany had been the decisive consideration. The position of the United States remained clear and simple: President Wilson had no love for the Bolsheviks, but through his experience in Mexico he was disillusioned with the idea of intervening in other countries' civil conflicts. He wished to get U.S. forces out of North Russia as soon as possible, and out of Siberia as soon as it could be assured that the Japanese would not grab the area. The far more war-weary British and French followed more ambiguous policies.

The French leaders favored destroying the Soviets and launched a major intervention in South Russia, landing French and Greek troops at Odessa soon after the armistice with Germany. This operation took place much against the recommendation of the commanders involved, who knew their men were not up to it. Brilliant Soviet propaganda undermined the morale of the tired and bewildered French, resulting in a mutiny in the fleet. The troops ashore had to be hastily withdrawn in 1919 before the Red Army got to close quarters and a total disaster occurred. The principal effect of the French intervention was to provide the Reds with a large quantity of supplies, abandoned during the evacuation. After this the French still favored destroying the Communist regime—but with other people's soldiers.

The British government's position was crucial, but it was badly divided. The clever and far-sighted Minister of Munitions, Winston Churchill, and a few other leaders favored an all-out effort to destroy the Soviet regime. Churchill warned that a great "Jacobin" military empire would be a permanent danger to the West. At the other extreme the Labour party, although not liking the Communists, opposed intervention. Lloyd George, the slippery Liberal Prime Minister of the wartime coalition government, wavered between dreams of breaking up the Russian empire into its national components and proto-McCarthyite smears of Labour as "Bolshevist." Basically, though, he was hostile to the Whites and favored withdrawal. Most of the cabinet, however, felt that considerations of honor if not interest bound Britain to support the Whites to some degree. It was agreed in late 1918 to keep British forces in North Russia, move some British troops into the Transcaucasus area to replace the departing German and Turkish forces, and supply the Whites with arms and advisors. Later, a single R. A. F. squadron was assigned to support Denikin. No new theater of intervention would be opened, however. Except for the disastrous French landing on the Black Sea coast, Allied troops after the armistice continued to face the Soviets only in the minor northern theater, where no decisive results could be expected.

The Allies' decisions took place in an atmosphere of war-weariness far deeper than that after 1945; yet that alone cannot explain their failure to take decisive action against the Bolsheviks, whose basic hostility to the West was already abundantly clear. Even in 1919 the British and French governments found possible forces for military operations in Afghanistan, Morocco, and Syria, for the attempt to impose a harsh peace on Turkey, and the effort to crush the Irish Revolution. The truth of the matter was that the issue in Russia either did not seem very important or, blinded by various diversionary formulas, the Western leaders and peoples convinced themselves that the outcome of the Russian Civil War was really none of their business, or at least not for them to determine. As R. H. Ullman has brilliantly observed, "Lloyd George and Woodrow Wilson's position was that if the Whites really *deserved* to win they would be able to do so by attracting the mass of the Russian population. Here was a fundamentally fallacious analogy—that a civil war was like an especially violent election from which the party that can attract the most popular support will emerge victorious."[9] In 1919 the Western leaders even launched an attempt to settle the Civil War by negotiation, which collapsed of its own absurdity. The analogy, which Ullman summarized, had a tremendous lifespan and inflicted an unbelievable amount of confusion and harm on the Western democracies and their friends. It and the kind of thinking it represented showed a strange tendency to see the institutions and achievements of Western democratic society in places and situations which they did not exist and simultaneously devaluated them. Churchill was wiser, but as in so much of his career, he was in the position of the one-eyed man in the country of the blind.

Churchill later felt that the armistice with Germany had been the "death warrant" of the White cause.[10] Yet the Whites still had a fair chance of victory in 1919. They were to squander this by strategic misjudgment, mismanagement, and lack of discipline.

Admiral Kolchak was recognized by the Allies and General Denikin as the nominal leader of the Whites. But he never exerted any influence outside Siberia and often did not have much real control even there. Although he managed to build up a well-armed force of 130,000 men, his supply system never functioned well. Kolchak was a poor administrator and knew little about land warfare; he relied on ambitious junior officers to run the military campaign.

In the spring of 1919 he launched an offensive. To the extent there was one, the main effort was mistakenly directed northwest toward Viatka through dense forests and swamps; Kolchak hoped to join up with the British forces in North Russia. In fact there would have been little value in such a junction, whereas an attack directed to the southwest would at least have threatened the rear of the forces facing Denikin. Kolchak's own rear areas were in bad shape. The Siberian peasants had been little affected by the Soviet regime and saw little reason to fight. The coup of November 1918 had caused some Socialist Revolutionaries to go over to the Red side, while others went underground to launch a futile struggle against both sides. Resentment against the draft and forced requisitions led to guerrilla fighting in the White rear. Although not very numerous in Kolchak's area, non-Russian nationalities occupied some strategic locations and were increasingly shaky. The flexible Soviet nationalities policy allowed the Communists to win over the previously anticommunist Bashkirs, who defected to the Red Army in February 1919. Later the Kazakhs did the same.

After initial victories in March and April the Whites were stopped. In late April the Soviets went over to the offensive. By August the Soviets had captured the Ural region, the only developed area in Kolchak's command. After this the White front in the east rapidly disintegrated. The remnants of Kolchak's forces and hordes of refugees fled eastward.[11]

The real threat to the Soviet regime in 1919 came from Denikin in the south. Skillfully shuttling troops back and forth, Denikin threw back attacks on the lower Don and Donetz areas. With helpful pressure from the British, Ataman Krasnov was persuaded to accept subordination to Denikin early in 1919; later the Cossacks became disillusioned with Krasnov and replaced him with an Ataman more cooperative with the White leaders. The Cossacks of the northern Don, who had given up the struggle for a time, were disillusioned by their second taste of Communist rule and rose up behind the Soviet lines. In the spring of 1919 the whole of the Don was liberated, and Denikin's forces began advancing north. On July 1 the easternmost White force, Baron Wrangel's Caucasian Army, managed to take Tsaritsyn—although the decisive role was played by a single tank manned by British advisors taking part in the battle against orders from the War Office.

Denikin had an apparently secure base of support in southern Russia and abundant supplies from the British. His command was now organized as a group of "armies"—Volunteer, Don, and Caucasian, plus several smaller "groups." But all these forces put together did not equal a single field army of the world war. Denikin was now ready to launch a decisive blow with the support of a small White army in Estonia organized with British help under the command of General Yudenich. He would attempt to capture Petrograd. It was clear to both sides that the coming campaign would decide the Civil War. The Reds had the advantage of superior numbers and a central position that contained most of Russia's productive capacity and population. The White forces were better led and better supplied, and they had a better cavalry arm, as well as some tanks. They also controlled an area that, unlike the areas under Soviet rule, had a surplus of food. But while both sides were widely hated—the mass of Russian peasants just wanted to be left alone—the divisions on the White side ran far deeper and were uncontrolled by the discipline and faith exerted by the Communist party.

The Whites in the south remained heavily dependent on the Don and Kuban Cossacks, who throughout the war formed a majority of the men in the White ranks. The Kuban Cossack leaders were continuously at odds with Denikin and his generals and demanded at least substantial autonomy in a future Russia. And after Kaledin no Cossack leader had the courage or foresight to try to reconcile the *inogorodny*, who remained hostile to the White cause; most of the cavalrymen on the Red side were drawn from this group. The White leaders did not have the will, or perhaps the power, to intervene in Cossack affairs in favor of the *inogorodny*. The White base in the south thus remained fundamentally flawed.

The White leaders' reluctance to quarrel with the Cossacks over this issue was understandable. But in addition to the problem this created, their administration of the areas under their control was poor and they had no policies for the areas they expected to occupy. General Denikin was a liberal, close to the Cadet party in his personal views, and an admirer of Britain and France. Yet he was constrained by legalistic qualms in his approach to political questions, and he knew that many, perhaps most, of the officers in his army were far more conservative than he was. (The Cossacks—on matters other than their relationship with the *inogorodny*—were often surprisingly far to the left.) Denikin was unwilling to provoke a major dispute about the future of Russia. The Whites only slowly worked out an inadequate policy on the land question. Unwilling simply to legalize the peasants' seizure of the land, probably the only realistic thing to do, they decided to let the peasants provisionally retain the land and pay rent on it until a final settlement was worked out. Although Denikin was supported by the rightmost Russian socialists, he failed to win over the Mensheviks, who might have brought over the support of much of the working class. Nor did the Whites have a policy on the nationalities problem. Devoted to a united Russia and hobbled by a devotion to legalism, Denikin refused to promise anything to the non-Russian nationalities. He refused an offer of alliance from the Ukrainian nationalist leaders in July 1919, and he let his subordinates tie up troops in a border conflict with Georgia, which had already established its independence under a Menshevik government, and in attempts to pacify Daghestan in the far south.

Overestimating his own strength, Denikin thought the Reds were far weaker than they in fact were. He was unable to credit the Communists with any ability, remarking that all they had done was to "destroy the bourgeoisie, disorganize society, and dishonor the name of Russia." His order for the final offensive, the "Moscow Directive" issued on July 3, seems to have been based on the assumption that the Reds were already collapsing. It envisaged a dangerous dispersal of forces. The main effort, to be carried out by the core of the old Volunteer Army, was to go up the Donetz through Kursk and Orel to Moscow. The other White forces would fan out over a huge area from west of the Dnieper to the Volga.

The Reds rated Kolchak as a more serious threat and concentrated on pursuing his broken forces, but they were badly disorganized in the south. In the Ukraine their rear areas were torn up by peasant guerrillas. Denikin was able to roll back the Red Army on a broad front and occupy a large area, which did give him the chance to draft new men for his forces. However, he failed to inflict a decisive defeat on the enemy, and venturesome subordinates dispersed his forces even more than he had planned. The White forces in the Ukraine pushed far to the west, tying up troops fighting the nationalists.

Nevertheless, the Communists feared they were on the brink of defeat. By October 1919 the White forces had taken Orel, just 250 miles from Moscow. The commander of the southern front, A. I. Egorov, warned Moscow that any further retreat threatened his command with complete disintegration. The Communists embarked on a last-ditch effort to mobilize every bit of military potential to stop the Whites in the south and before Petrograd. Heroic efforts supplied the Red Army with its first crude tanks for the Petrograd front, and Communist party members were hastily herded to the front to galvanize resistance. Once hustled out of the Ukraine, the Soviets had a stable rear. The peasants of Russia proper had already risen against their new masters and been beaten in 1918; now they were broken to harness.

The Whites had dispersed their strength and were unable to make use of the areas they had taken. Denikin had to make use of old-government officials and military officers to run the captured areas. In a situation that was completely unfamiliar, they often did not know what to do and, more restorationist than Denikin, tried to bring back the landlords. Denikin failed to discipline his forces. Except in Wrangel's army—Wrangel ruthlessly maintained discipline by hanging and flogging where necessary—violence and looting were widespread. Large numbers of Don Cossacks left the front to take their loot home. Typifying an atmosphere of paranoia, unrealism, and scapegoating, anti-Semitism was widespread and violent in the White forces. Although not an anti-Semite himself, Denikin was forced to dismiss the few Jewish officers in his army; he also failed to stop bloody pogroms in the Ukraine. The massacres committed by the White forces were probably not as great as those committed by the Ukrainians; nonetheless the Jews, who at first had welcomed the Whites as liberators, learned to flee with the retreating Red forces. Raids by Ukrainian anarchists seriously interfered with the rail system. Corruption and misconduct were common in the rear areas. British supplies, which the British mistakenly turned over to the Whites without close supervision, were often stolen. (The Americans were to make exactly the same mistake in China and Indochina.) The Whites had only military momentum to sustain them by October 1919.

As Nicolai Yudenich's tiny Northwestern Army tried and failed to storm Petrograd, the Soviets amassed a force of 177,000 men against perhaps 98,000 Whites on the front line and launched a double counterblow in the south. They struck at the spearhead of the Volunteer Army at Orel. It fell back in good order, but the right flank of the White front was torn open. The new First Cavalry Army, which concentrated the best Red horsemen into one powerful force with its own supporting planes, artillery, armored cars, and armored trains broke through the Don Cossack Army near Voronezh. The Whites were routed, and the defeat on the upper Don unhinged their whole front. When the final victory they had expected and so desperately counted upon failed to materialize, and defeat occurred instead, the Whites' morale went to pieces. They fell back into the Crimea and behind the Don so fast that the Reds, impeded by miserable weather and a half-ruined railroad system, found it difficult to keep up with them or maintain a strong force at the front. The Soviets continued to advance although they were now at the end of a long and tenuous supply line and no longer had much of a numerical advantage. In January 1920 Rostov fell; the Kuban Cossacks began to desert. Denikin's forces began to disintegrate; amid scenes of horror part of the White forces and a horde of refugees were evacuated from the North Caucasus to the Crimea. Now discredited, Denikin turned over his command to General Wrangel.

A baron of Baltic German and Swedish origin, Wrangel was in temperament and convictions far more conservative than Denikin, the son of a serf. But he was also a realist and was far readier to try "progressive" policies, in his words, "to make a left policy with right hands"—notably on the land issue. He was also tough-minded and ready to do what was needed to maintain discipline. He established a relatively efficient administration and army in the

Crimea. Although Wrangel's problems were in some ways more manageable than Denikin's—as a well-known and trusted conservative he could not be pressured by the right, which in any case was now desperate enough to try anything—he showed what might have been achieved earlier. When Poland attacked the Soviets in April 1920, Wrangel broke out of the Crimea, pushing into the Ukraine and attempting a landing in the Kuban. The odds against him were now overwhelming, however; the tiny beachhead in the Crimea was not enough of a base against the now consolidated regime. When the war with Poland petered out into a stalemate, the Soviets committed all their power against Wrangel. The Whites were forced to evacuate.[12]

After the end of the Civil War the Soviets still faced a crisis. The policy of War Communism might have kept the army adequately supplied, but the economy was in ruins. There was much discontent even among the most fervent supporters of the regime; this culminated in a rebellion by the sailors of the Baltic Fleet at Kronstadt. A new wave of peasant rebellions broke out in southern and central Russsia. A terrible famine in 1921–22 caused 5 *million* deaths; part of the Volga region was reduced to cannibalism. The Soviets secured from the United States large-scale aid that saved several million lives and possibly averted the collapse of the regime. Lenin resolved the overall problem by belatedly introducing a number of steps, long advocated by the Mensheviks, under the name of the "New Economic Policy" or NEP. The NEP was primarily an accommodation with the peasantry. The forced requisitions of agricultural produce were replaced by a smaller, graduated tax in kind. The peasants' rights to buy and sell the rest of what they grew were recognized. The NEP also legalized small-scale capitalism and private trade; some small enterprises were leased to private owners or cooperatives.

But Lenin strongly opposed any real liberalization; he rejected the idea that freedom be extended to non-Bolshevik socialist groups or that the Communist party itself be "democratized." Instead, the Legal Opposition was crushed at the very moment when the economic ideas of the Mensheviks were being implemented.[13] The totalitarian character of the Soviet government was thus actually strengthened while there took place a retreat on the economic front and a certain limited accommodation with the outside world. This was no accident, but the first instance of a pattern. At least until Stalin's death, the Soviet state characteristically followed relatively moderate and tolerant policies when under strong pressure from the outside, as, for example, during part of the Civil War and World War II, and cracked down on its subjects when the external danger lessened. Nor did moves at accommodation with other states have any necessary relationship in that era, or even later, to internal liberalization. (Khrushchev was never more "liberal" than in the tense years of 1961–62, whereas he backtracked when détente with the United States began in 1963.)

Despite their nominal belief in the supremacy of economic matters, Lenin and his successors in the Soviet Union and elsewhere actually placed their primary emphasis on preserving and extending their political control. Moreover, it was tacitly recognized that War Communism had been a mistake, or at least was not desirable to repeat; future Communist regimes did not try to create a command economy at such reckless speed.

The NEP was widely misinterpreted outside the Soviet Union as the beginning of a restoration of capitalism. Many pundits in the West prophesied that the Russian Revolution would experience a turn to the right or normalization, as had the French Revolution. If this happened at all, however, it was only in a very limited way. It was a concession to reality, decreed by the ruling group, which did not affect the main results of the revolution.

By 1921 the Soviets had secured control over the core of the old Russian empire. Yet it was a victory, due almost as much to the Whites' failures and the blunders of the Western powers as their own strength. The mistakes of the Whites have already been discussed; however, those of the Western powers are of at least equal interest. Lenin himself admitted that had the Western powers sent a force of hundreds of thousands of men, a force, in other words, no greater than that committed by the Americans in the Korean War, they would have defeated the Soviet regime. He maintained that their failure to do so showed the internal decay of capitalism. Even a much lesser commitment of the sort envisaged by Winston Churchill, a volunteer force emphasizing aircraft and armor, might well have turned the tide. The British military historian Liddell Hart remarked that the capture of Tsaritsyn suggested that "the course of history might have been changed by quite a small British armoured force, properly organized, even on the basis possible in 1919."[14] The Allies failed to act on the proposals of the Yugoslav and Bulgarian governments, each of which offered to send a corps of 30,000–40,000 men to Russia if the Allies were willing to transport and supply them.[15]

For whatever reasons—war-weariness, disinterest in Russian affairs, or sheer confusion about what was going on —the Western democracies expended hundreds of thousands of lives to defeat Imperial Germany but failed to prevent the rise of a regime that was far worse, and far more inimical to them, in the ruins of Imperial Russia. Churchill admirably summarized the Allies' bungling: "Were they at war with Soviet Russia? Certainly not, but they shot Soviet Russians on sight. They armed the enemies of the Soviet Government. They blockaded its ports and sank its battleships. They earnestly desired and schemed its downfall. But war—shocking! Interference—shame! It was, they repeated, a matter of indifference to them how Russians settled their own affairs. They were impartial—bang! And then, at the same time— parley and try to trade."[16] All this foreshadowed the clumsy, hit-or-miss, and generally ineffective use of force that marked the Western powers' handling of most of the small wars after 1945.

Yet the intervention had not been entirely without effect. Whereas the American-Japanese effort in Eastern Siberia actually had the effect of assisting the Soviet regime, the British effort in European Russia did prolong the Civil War. It helped to prevent the Soviets from assisting the short-lived Communist regime in Hungary and from reconquering some of the western territories of the old Russian empire. It is sometimes claimed that the intervention boomeranged and roused nationalist sentiments in favor of the Soviet regime, but there is little evidence that anything like this happened except in Siberia. If Russians were not aroused to a patriotic frenzy by the presence of huge German and Austrian forces in some of the most important areas of their country in 1917–18, it is hardly likely that they were much upset by the presence of small Allied forces in peripheral areas in 1918–19. Even in Siberia people were upset not by the mere arrival of the Japanese but by their outrageous behavior.

Nevertheless, the Allied intervention did have a significant drawback. Although it did not in fact represent an all-out effort by the rest of the world to destroy the Soviet regime—that was not even the Allied aim until November 1918—it was easy for the Soviets to misrepresent it as such. The propaganda surrounding the intervention varied greatly over the years. Between the world wars the Soviets stressed the role of Britain, France, and Japan, which during most of that era happened to be the main threats to the Soviet Union or the main obstacles to its expansion. It was admitted at the time that American actions in Siberia had actually worked in favor of Soviet interests. After World War II the official record was revised to make the United States a prime villain.[17] When the intervention was recalled in the West, it was seen as an embarrassment. Curiously, it was often treated as more significant than the larger issue of the Russian Civil War. Western historians raked over the history of the intervention again and again but paid little attention to the struggle among the Russians themselves until the 1960s.

Thus ended disastrously the first war between the Western democracies and the Soviets—for unintentional and bungling as the West's military operations were, they did constitute a war. But only the Soviets fully realized that there had been a war, and drew lessons from it. The episodes of Brest-Litovsk, the Civil War and intervention, and the concurrent efforts to retake the old Russian empire and launch the world revolution (to be discussed in following chapters) helped form the basic characteristics of the Soviet approach to foreign relations. The Soviets realized that they could do much as they pleased within the boundaries of the old empire without being called to account, except perhaps in a few border areas. As long as they exercised some prudence in the use of military force outside those boundaries, they could combine the pursuit of world revolution with normal diplomatic and trade relations with the capitalist countries. Rivalries between the capitalist countries, which Soviet diplomacy could manipulate, internal divisions within them, and the basic decadence of their ruling groups would prevent any really effective action against the Soviets.

Many in the West contented themselves with the fact that communism had been contained within the boundaries of the Russian empire. Contrary to Bolshevik expectations, no successful revolutions took place in the West. As we shall see, there had in fact been little if any chance for this. The actual results were bad enough. The second most numerous of the Western peoples, talented and enduring, had fallen under the rule of a totalitarian regime unalterably hostile to the Western democracies.

The Reconquest of the Russian Empire

Count Witte, one of the last great statesmen of Imperial Russia, once wrote (ironically in the context of attacking extreme Russian chauvinism): "There is no Russia, there is only the Russian empire." The truth of this statement was amply demonstrated during and after the revolution, and the Communists, whatever their promises and propaganda, acted as though it were true. The Civil War among the Russians themselves overlapped and was entangled with the Soviet government's largely successful attempt to bring the whole of the former empire under its rule. And at first the Communists' effort to reconquer the empire was not clearly distinguishable from their effort to promote world revolution.

On Lenin's insistence, despite considerable opposition, the Bolsheviks had accepted a program insisting on the absolute right of "self-determination" for all nationalities. During 1917 this promise helped the Bolsheviks to either neutralize or obtain alliances with most of the non-Russian nationalities. Rather reluctantly, Lenin also adopted the idea of a federal form for the future Russian state. This idea, like the Bolshevik land policy, was adapted from the platform of the Socialist Revolutionaries and was designed to attract the non-Russians and discourage them from actually seeking separation from Russia once the Bolsheviks had taken power. These promises provided the basis for an extremely elastic policy that permitted the Communists both to form alliances with various nationalist groups against the Whites and to conquer them by force when the situation seemed ripe—for it was up to the leaders in Moscow to decide *who* was legitimately seeking self-determination. It was always possible to discover that the popular will was "really" being expressed by the local Communists or some splinter group willing to obey Moscow.[1] As already noted, in the case of the Ukraine the Communists twice allied themselves with the Ukrainian nationalists and then, backing the local Communists, turned against them. As the Soviets pursued the beaten White armies in 1919–20, the Ukraine was reoccupied in a simple military operation and the guerrillas gradually wiped out.

When the world war ended in 1918, Lenin had viewed the reconquest of the Ukraine and the Baltic States as reopening the way to the West. On December 24, 1918, the Soviet government recognized the independence of the "Soviet Republics" of Estonia, Latvia, and Lithuania, which were still under nominal German occupation or nationalist control, and promised aid to them. *Izvestiya* commented that the three Baltic countries "are directly on the road from Russia to Western Europe and are therefore a hindrance to our revolution because they separate Soviet Russia from revolutionary Germany. This separating wall has to be destroyed. The Russian Red proletariat should find an opportunity to influence the revolution in Germany."[2] As the Germans left, the Red Army marched west. The Estonians held out, but farther south the Red Army quickly drove to the Baltic, overrunning most of Latvia and part of Lithuania. In Latvia communism had a genuine if short-lived popularity, and there an effective Communist administration was set up. It professed to be the government of an "independent" Latvia only because Lenin insisted on this as part of his long-term political strategy. But the successful defense of Estonia left the Soviet position in the Baltic States a dangerously exposed salient, and the Red Army was increasingly preoccupied elsewhere. Latvian nationalist forces aided by the British and assisted by a German volunteer corps formed from elements of the former occupation forces managed to drive the Soviets out of Latvia while the Poles drove them out of Lithuania.[3]

In the largely Moslem southern regions of the old empire, Central Asia and the Caucasus, Soviet rule was successfully established, but only after a long and complicated struggle.

In 1917 Central Asia was divided between Russian Turkestan, under direct Russian rule, and two native protectorates, Bukhara and Khiva, which the Imperial government had largely left to their own devices. Turkestan had a considerable minority of Russian settlers and workers as well as colonial administrators. The area and the Russian role there rather resembled French Northwest Africa. The Moslem natives, whose nationalist sentiments grew rapidly in 1917, had little sympathy for the Provisional Government. They were mostly passive during the Bolshevik Revolution, which met little resistance in Turkestan. Russians of all classes were conscious of their isolation and wished to maintain a common front against the natives. The Moslem nationalist organizations and the Russians' Turkestan Soviet coexisted uneasily for a time. Then in December the Moslem National People's Council at Kokand declared the autonomy of Turkestan. In January 1918 the Tashkent Soviet sent Russian troops to take Kokand; the nationalists were smashed. (Simultaneously the Soviet authorities suppressed the nationalist organizations of the Tatars and the Bashkirs in the Crimea and the Volga and Ural areas.) Then the Soviets turned against Bukhara. There the emir, a reactionary tyrant, was trying to crush the local reformers, the "Young Bukharans," who formed an alliance with the Soviets. But a Soviet attack on Bukhara in March 1918 failed. The Soviets had successfully smashed the modernist nationalist movement in Turkestan, but not the reactionary and religious opposition. Moslem guerrillas called "Basmachis" soon limited Soviet control to Tashkent and a few other spots. The Soviet regime continued to rest almost solely on the support of the Russian minority; it was in fact a thinly disguised perpetuation of the old colonial administration and its abuses. Moslems were almost entirely excluded from Soviet institutions. The White conquest of Siberia soon cut Turkestan off from the rest of Soviet

Russia. A small British force moved into Transcaspia in the extreme southwest in order to prevent a Turkish advance across the Caspian; with its help a short-lived White Russian regime was formed in that area.

The Turkestan Soviet held out against considerable odds until the defeat of Kolchak reopened the Moscow-Tashkent railroad in September 1919. Lenin was disgusted to learn of the misconduct of the Tashkent regime. Increasingly interested in revolution in Asia, he quickly acted to reform the Soviet administration in Central Asia. He regarded the Soviet regime there as an important showpiece with which to attract Asian support for communism. He described it as "gigantic and world historical in importance": "For all of Asia, and for all of the colonies of the world, for a thousand million people, the relations of the Soviet worker-peasant republic to the weak, hitherto oppressed peoples, will have a practical significance." He stressed its importance for the "supreme struggle with world imperialism headed by Britain."[4] This attributed an excessive importance to Central Asia. In reality the peoples and nationalist movements of Asia and Africa continued to know and care remarkably little about what went on there, which was a good thing for the Soviet Union. The work of suppressing the Basmachis was not finished until 1936.

As Turkestan was brought under Soviet control, the Red Army got ready in 1920 for a new and better-prepared attack on Bukhara and Khiva. Khiva was an easy target. It was torn by civil war between the nomadic Turkomen and the settled peoples, and a liberal "Young Khivan" party was willing to help the Soviets against their traditional rulers. Khiva was quickly conquered.

Some of the leftmost Young Bukharan exiles in Soviet Tashkent had broken with their old comrades, and formed a Bukharan Communist party. The Red Army attacked Bukhara in August 1920 with minor help from an uprising organized by the Bukharan Communists. The emir's capital, largely defended by Afghan mercenaries, was stormed on September 1. Bukhara and Khiva, the latter renamed Khorezm, were quickly reorganized as "People's Soviet Republics." They became the first fully successful

Soviet puppet regimes. In 1923 they joined the newly formed
Soviet Union. Shortly thereafter they were abolished when the
whole Central Asia region was reorganized along "national" lines,
forming five member republics in the Soviet Union.[5]

In the Caucasus things were more complicated. The region was
a tangle of mutually hostile peoples not amenable to direct control
by Moscow. In March 1918 the Soviets founded the first Soviet
puppet state, the Terek People's Soviet Socialist Republic, to
control an area north of the main Caucasus range. It had a mixed
population of Terek Cossacks, *inogorodny*, and Caucasian moun-
tain people. The Communists retained control of the government,
but they maintained a nominal coalition with socialist and even
liberal groups at a time when these were being suppressed in the
rest of the country. The regime soon collapsed when the Terek
Cossacks joined the White side in the Civil War and the Ingush
tribesmen began attacking Russians whatever their politics. The
area was finally taken by the Red Army and made part of the
Russian Soviet Socialist Republic.

Farther south the Transcaucasian peoples, the Armenians, Geor-
gians, and Azerbaijanis, established their independence after the
Bolshevik Revolution. The three countries tried to form a federa-
tion, but national hatreds, particularly violent between the Armenians and Azerbaijanis, quickly tore it apart. In April 1918 the
local Soviet seized control of the oil center of Baku, the multinational capital of Azerbaijan; but it was unable to take over the rest
of the country. During 1918 Armenia and Azerbaijan were briefly
overrun by Turkish forces, which installed the Azerbaijani nationalists in power at Baku. Georgia was ruled by the Georgian
branch of the Mensheviks and briefly came under German occupation. After the collapse of the Central Powers, British forces
occupied Georgia and Baku for a short time. They left the local
institutions undisturbed and withdrew in the summer of 1919,
exposing the area to Soviet conquest. As the Civil War came to an
end, the Soviets found the conquest of Transcaucasia easy. Azerbaijan and Armenia were at war with each other. When the Red
Army marched into Azerbaijan in April 1920, it met little resist-

ance. The Armenians were also at war with the Turks, who had recently exterminated a large part of the Armenian people; in December 1920 they submitted to Soviet rule almost without a fight as the lesser of two evils. Georgia, by far the best run of the Transcaucasian lands, was a tougher target. Its Menshevik government was well-known and liked in the West. Lenin was a bit reluctant to embark on a new conflict that would cause bad publicity abroad. But Josef Stalin, a Georgian Communist who was increasingly influential, persuaded him to launch an attack. A minor peasant uprising organized by the not very strong Georgian Communist party was seized on as "proof" that the Georgian government was unpopular and oppressive. In February 1921 the Red Army marched in. Turkey, then a Soviet ally, joined in the attack and annexed a small area of Georgia.[6]

During the reconquest of the Russian empire the Soviets developed many devices later used in expansion beyond the border of the Soviet Union, and the experience had an important effect on the thinking of the Soviet leaders and on Communists in general. The often foolish, and even suicidal, actions of the nationalists among Russia's subject peoples powerfully contributed to the Communists' rather exaggerated contempt for "bourgeois" nationalists in Asia and Africa. It promoted the conviction that in the long run the Soviet Union and/or the local Communists would outmaneuver their non-Communist rivals. The Russian Communists had found it remarkably easy to ally themselves with, cheat, and split nationalist groups. Ultimately the leadership of the groups opposing the Communists had tended to fall into the hands of reactionaries or people more preoccupied with hatred of other nationalities than with opposing the Soviets.

Nationalism in the Russian empire proved mainly a destructive force. The nationalism of the non-Russians was sometimes an obstacle to the Communists, but more often it worked in their favor by dividing the ranks of their enemies. The various subject peoples often hated each other as much or more than they did the Russians. The popular notion that nationalism or nationalist movements constitute a stumbling block to communism had little reality in the

Russian empire in 1917–21. Whether the notion has been true anywhere else is at least questionable—quite apart from the fact that during and after World War II a number of Communist parties, notably the Chinese, Yugoslav, and Vietnamese, were themselves able to become the embodiment of nationalist sentiment and ride it to supreme power.

In one area of Russia itself Lenin chose to create a peculiar satellite state for diplomatic reasons. In 1920 the Red Army approached the part of Siberia occupied by Japan. The Soviets created a "Far Eastern Republic" in April 1920 to keep a "buffer" between the Soviet state and the Japanese, which might be useful in maneuvering between Japan and the United States. It was a nominal coalition regime, including Socialist Revolutionaries and Mensheviks, but was headed by a reliable Communist official. Its armed forces were always under the direct control of the Red Army. For a time Lenin hoped that the Far Eastern Republic might assist him in provoking a Japanese-American war. (He publicly referred to this idea with such glee that even other Communists were shocked.) This did not materialize, at least not in the 1920s, but the Far Eastern Republic proved of some help in obtaining Japan's evacuation of Siberia in November 1922. Its usefulness exhausted, the republic was incorporated into the Russian Soviet Republic.[7]

All these actions foreshadowed or helped to perfect the methods Stalin was to use in conquering the empire he was to acquire during and after World War II.

World Revolution

Despite the Civil War, during 1918 Lenin paid minute attention to foreign developments that seemed to affect the still-expected revolution in Europe. In a struggle for the allegiance of the world socialist movement, he waged a war of words with Karl Kautsky, the leading Marxist theoretician of the age. While Kautsky vigorously attacked the Bolsheviks in the name of democracy, Lenin counterattacked, justifying Bolshevik policies and his own interpretation of the "dictatorship of the proletariat." The Russian Communists sent some agents abroad and channeled money, propaganda, and even arms to the German Spartacists, the only revolutionary group to which they had ready access. But as yet they had no real organization or means of exerting much influence in other countries. Lenin often showed a remarkable understanding of the internal politics of the left and the problems of organizing revolution. Yet he failed to really appreciate the differences between Russia and the rest of Europe, differences that made a repetition of the October Revolution unlikely if not impossible. Only fantastic blunders by the Allies made a brief Communist seizure of power in Hungary possible. Lenin's mistakes were perhaps not incomprehensible, however, for in Finland, a borderland between Russia and West, an extension of the Bolshevik Revolution nearly occurred.

Before World War I Finland had been an autonomous part of the Russian empire, with a political system far more liberal than that in Russia itself. Finland resembled Scandinavia and Western Europe much more than Russia, but the Russian Revolution had a great effect on the country. Most Finns strongly resented Russian rule, and a strong Social Democratic party expressed fierce resentments by workers and tenant farmers against the heavily Swedish upper class. The Germans had organized a "Jaeger" battalion of Finnish volunteers to fight against Russia. After the downfall of the tsar sentiment in favor of independence grew stronger. In April 1917 a secret military committee organized a civic guard or "Protective Corps" for a possible independence struggle. At first it was supported by the Social Democrats, and railroad workers helped steal Russian weapons for it. The committee contacted the Germans, who finally sent the Protective Corps a shipload of arms, which was brought ashore in the confused situation preceding the Bolshevik Revolution. By this time the Social Democrats had broken with the other Finnish parties, who dominated the government, narrowly losing the elections held in October 1917. In late November the country was still occupied by pro-Bolshevik Russian troops, and Lenin urged the Finnish Social Democrats to follow his example and seize power. The Finnish Social Democrats, however, had never split along the lines of their Russian counterparts. Although a "Red Guard" had been set up with Russian help to counter the Protective Corps, which was dominated by non-socialists, most of the Social Democratic leaders were reluctant to see a civil war. The middle-class government of Prime Minister Pehr Svinhufvud declared Finland independent on December 6. Despite grumbling about being forced to deal with a "bourgeois" government, Lenin recognized the Finnish regime on December 31, possibly hoping that this would discourage the Germans from taking action in Finland. The Russian forces stayed, however, and the leaders of the Red Guard, a well-armed force of 30,000 men, agitated for an uprising. Against Social Democratic opposition Svinhufvud decided to expel the Russian forces. He sent Gustav Mannerheim, an able Imperial Russian army general with only a loose connection with Finland, to secure a base for the government forces in conservative northern Finland. Unplanned clashes between the Protective Corps and Red Guards, helped by Russians, began at Vyborg (Viipuri) on January 19. On January 23 the Finnish government openly demanded a Russian withdrawal. On the same day the Soviet commissar for war ordered the Russian troops in Finland to disarm the Protective Corps, apparently without any coordination with the Red Guard. The Russians were so demoralized and disorganized by this time that little happened; in some cases "White" Finns disarmed them instead! Under German pressure the Russians were then ordered to stay neutral. The Red Guard leaders finally bluntly told the nominal leaders of the Soviet Democrats that they would start a revolution with or without their consent. Most of the Social Democratic leaders reluctantly bowed to this pressure, but some went over to Svinhufvud's government instead. On January 27–28 the Red Guards overthrew the government in southern Finland. With very small forces General Mannerheim promptly disarmed the Russian troops in his area, who offered little effective resistance. They were his main source of arms. He quickly overran much of Finland, while White forces in the south began guerrilla operations.

The Red Finns foolishly remained passive, building up their forces in the south with Russian help and eliminating White pockets there. The Red Finnish regime was never a full-blown Communist state. A Finnish Communist party was organized only in August 1918. Although a small-scale Red Terror was launched, moderate socialists retained some influence. Morale on the Red side was low, and the Whites found that the workers they drafted proved loyal. By fighting a daring war of movement, Mannerheim was able to defeat superior forces. In February the Germans returned the Jaeger battalion to Finland and shipped captured Russian weapons to the White Finns. On February 21, despite Mannerheim's opposition, Svinhufvud secured a German promise to intervene in force. The Whites were joined by a Swedish volunteer brigade.

The Treaty of Brest-Litovsk forced the Russian troops to evacuate Finland. But a volunteer force of 1,000 men stayed behind to give the Red Finns advice and specialized support, although there was severe friction between the two nationalities. The Reds built up a well-armed force of 90,000–100,000 men, but they were poorly organized and lacked any able commanders. A Red offensive in early March was defeated. Having built up a force of 50,000–60,000 men, Mannerheim was determined to win a decisive victory before the Germans came or the Baltic ice thawed and allowed the Russian fleet to operate against him. He skillfully cut off the bulk of the Red forces in western Finland, winning a great victory at Tampere on April 5. This, and not the intervention of the Germans, really decided the war; but a German division landed at Hango and advanced cautiously on Helsinki. Mannerheim then concentrated on preventing the Red Finns from retreating to the Russian frontier and regrouping to try again. At the cost of some hard fighting in late April, he was successful. The Finnish Civil War ended early in May. Red Finnish prisoners suffered considerably in prison camps during 1918—some 10,000 died—apparently the result of the government's giving them last priority in a time of a general food shortage. In any case the "White Terror," if it really existed, did not last very long. Amnesties began in October 1918. Finland became a firmly democratic country and most of the grievances on which the Red Finns had capitalized were eliminated.[1]

The defeat of the Reds had arguably been nearly accomplished. It was partly due to Mannerheim's remarkable leadership and the unfavorable international situation that forced the Russians to leave, and military weaknesses. Had discipline been restored among the Russian troops or had the Red Finns avoided some military mistakes, the Finnish Civil War might have ended differently. Communists could also plausibly argue that a true Communist party would have performed better than the hesitant and divided Red Finn leadership.

As Germany's defeat became apparent in October 1918, Lenin declared that a revolution was imminent. He was confident that in a fairly short time it would take the same path as Russia's, and he called for preparations to support the German Revolution with an even larger Red Army than had previously been envisaged. At a time when Russia could hardly feed itself, he called for the creation of a reserve food supply for Germany—an idea that could not be carried out.

A revolution did take place in Germany, but it failed to take the form Lenin expected. A mutiny in the German fleet grew into a wild, spontaneous, and almost bloodless nationwide uprising. A system of soldiers' and workers' councils appeared as a democratic republic replaced the empire. But this was practically the end of the revolutionary process.

Some groups in Germany wanted the revolution to go farther. In April 1917 the German Social Democratic party had split over the issue of the war. The antiwar Independent Social Democrats included both right-wing and nonrevolutionary leftists. It also contained two revolutionary factions, the Revolutionary Shop Stewards and the more important Spartacist League. But a third, smaller group based in Bremen and outside the Independents formed the only real German counterpart of the Bolsheviks and were Lenin's only dependable followers in Germany. The main Spartacist leader, Rosa Luxemburg, though a supporter of violent revolution, was an old enemy of Lenin. She rejected his views on internal party organization and the party's relationship with the masses as undemocratic, and she disagreed with many Bolshevik policies and actions. Although the revolution of November 1918 had barely overtaken her group's planned uprising against the Imperial government, she quickly realized there was no prospect for an early "socialist" revolution. Only a minority of German workers were still in a revolutionary mood.

Nevertheless, the Spartacists became the core of the newly organized German Communist party. In a series of blunders the Communists let the Revolutionary Shop Stewards drag them into an attempt to seize power in Berlin in January 1919. The Social Democratic government smashed the uprising with army units and the help of "Free Corps" units composed of volunteers, mostly men of the far right. Luxemburg was killed after being captured. Another uprising by the far left took place in Bavaria in April. A group of semi-anarchist local extremists unconnected with the Communist party seized Munich. When this regime quickly fell apart, the local Communists, themselves only loosely connected to the Communist leadership in Berlin, took over; but they were quickly crushed. The effort to achieve a Communist revolution in Germany failed.

Despite a lost war and a disastrous economic situation, few Germans wanted a revolution. The soldiers' and workers' councils had remained in the hands of moderate socialists and never became instruments of class conflict; middle-class men, and even officers, were members of the councils. Although there was friction between the councils and the regular organs of government, this never became severe, and the councils finally peacefully dissolved. The government had never collapsed. The army's morale, though low, had not disintegrated. There was no revolutionary peasantry in Germany, and the overthrow of the Kaiser had coincided with the coming of peace; the war was thus no longer a live issue. The Social Democrats retained the loyalty of the workers, and they had no intention of committing the mistakes the democratic socialists had made in Russia. The whole political and social situation in Germany, in short, was quite different from that in Russia. The industrial workers in Germany formed a larger portion of society than did their counterparts in Russia; but so did the middle classes, and neither the workers nor peasants had any reason to welcome an extremist revolution. (Later events in Germany indicated that much of the middle class was more prone to political extremism than the workers—but this was not to benefit the Communists.) If this was true in Germany, despite the particularly bad conditions there, other advanced countries were bound to be even less susceptible to a Bolshevik-style revolution. However, the Communists convinced themselves that the postwar problems of the West were bound to grow worse, that its problems were insoluble, and they seized on the fact that the German Communists had not been properly organized and led along Leninist lines.[2] The revolution in Hungary briefly seemed to vindicate their optimism.

The Hungarian Communist party, unlike the German, stemmed from Soviet initiative, and its leaders had originated as Russian agents. Regarding Hungary as a target country second only to Germany, the Soviets had successfully indoctrinated many of the enormous number of Hungarian prisoners of war in Russia. On returning to Hungary in 1918, these men found a real revolutionary situation. Although a more advanced society than Imperial Russia, Hungary suffered sharp social cleavages. Despite the high degree of liberty in Hungary, the lower clases were disenfranchised, and parliament was carefully gerrymandered to reduce the influence of urban areas. The country was dominated by a clannish aristocracy that owned most of the land. The development of unions had been blocked outside of Budapest and some mining areas. Ethnic differences tended to coincide with class ones. Thus government jobs were monopolized by the Hungarian aristocracy, whereas the business and professional classes were largely Jewish and German; the lower classes were Christian Hungarians.

Defeat cost Hungary a large part of her territory and led to economic chaos. Hungary had lost much of her markets and raw materials, and there was enormous unemployment. There was general resentment against the shrunken frontiers being imposed on the country. The left-wing liberal government of Count Mihaly Karolyi, a man much like Kerensky but even more indecisive and unrealistic, was unable to improve the economic situation or introduce social reforms, especially the land reform desperately wanted by the peasantry. The Communist leader, Bela Kun, was a skillful propagandist who exploited the situation. Food shortages and the tendency toward radicalism of the large number of workers who had never been organized by the labor movement brought the Communists growing support. Violent demonstrations like those in Petrograd in July 1917 caused the government to jail the Communist leaders in February 1919.

The situation was already delicate when Allied blunders opened the door to the Communists. Giving in to the most exaggerated territorial claims of Hungary's neighbors, the Allied representative in Hungary, on March 20 ordered the Hungarians to give up a further slice of their territory, a purely Hungarian area containing Debrecen, the country's second largest city. The Hungarians were enraged. The Karolyi government, which had been friendly to the Allies, was finally discredited; it resigned, turning over power to the Social Democrats. The Social Democrats decided they could not rule alone while being undermined by the Communists. Like the country in general, they looked to an alliance with Russia as Hungary's last hope. The Social Democratic leaders met with Kun and his colleagues in their prison and agreed to form a government together, on Communist terms. The two parties fused into a single "Socialist party" under Kun's leadership and proclaimed a "Hungarian Soviet Republic." However, both sides had reservations about the agreement.

Lenin welcomed the revolution as an example of "peaceful transition," although he was not too pleased with Kun's deal with the Social Democrats, for his policy at this time was to draw the sharpest possible line between communism and democratic socialism. He warned Kun to beware of "Social Democratic treachery." But Kun was now ignoring his mentor. He hoped to outdo Lenin and achieve a faster transition to "socialism" than in Russia. He introduced policies similar to those of War Communism and rejected copying Lenin's policy of letting the peasants break up the great estates; instead the estates were to be preserved as state farms. The new regime was not really liked, but it stayed afloat on a wave of nationalist sentiment despite Kun's unwillingness to appeal openly to nationalism. He rejected a compromise territorial solution offered by General Jan Smuts of South Africa. War with Romania and Czechoslovakia resulted; those countries were firmly backed by the Allies, who were now really worried about the spread of communism. Romanian forces invaded what was left of Hungary, but a flood of workers left Budapest, forming a whole new army and hurling the Romanians back. The war effort was warmly supported by conservative nationalists. The Hungarians turned north; defeating the Czechs, they overran Slovakia, setting up a "Slovakian Soviet Republic" puppet state. On March 25 Lenin had ordered Soviet troops in the Ukraine to march against Romania to support the Hungarians. However, Denikin's successes and a mutiny of some Ukrainian units forced the Red Army to turn around. The Hungarian regime was thus isolated.

Even at the height of its military successes Kun's regime was shaky. There were constant peasant uprisings against food requisitioning, while the use of the printing press to generate money where needed led to a wild inflation. The distribution of food in Budapest broke down. Kun's violent campaign against religion alienated much of the population. Increasingly desperate, Kun decided that the Allied position toward his regime was now more moderate. He decided to retreat from Slovakia as a gesture. But the Allies did not react to this, and the regime became more unpopular. The nationalists were alienated, and the Social Democrats were unhappy. Kun tried to engineer a Communist coup in Austria, but this was a complete misfire. Amid an increasing wave of peasant rebellions, the army started to collapse as the Romanians counterattacked in July. As the Romanian army neared Budapest on August 1, the Communist leaders simply ran away. Social Democratic union leaders briefly took over the government, but the Romanians let a group of Hungarian "Whites" who had spent the period of Kun's rule skulking in complete safety in an Allied-occupied area overthrow the government. In Hungary, unlike Russia or Finland, the Whites were reactionaries pure and simple. They launched a reign of terror considerably bloodier than that of Kun's regime, with a strong admixture of anti-Semitism. (Kun and many of his colleagues were of Jewish origin.) As in Indonesia in 1965 and Chile in 1973, a group that had done little or nothing when the Communists were a real threat was guilty of the worst excesses when they were no longer a danger. Some 5,000 people were killed and 100,000 fled the country. After a while the terror subsided and the prewar status quo was gradually restored. The conservative regent, Admiral Horthy, who dominated Hungary until 1944, was not a man of high character, but under his governorship Hungary remained a free if in some ways rather backward country until it was occupied by the Nazis.

Lenin devoted considerable attention to the downfall of the Hungarian regime, which greatly affected the policies of the new Communist International. The Comintern criticized Kun for merging with the Social Democrats without proper guarantees and allegedly losing the Communist party's identity, for his failure to break up the estates, for not using patriotic appeals to keep the support of the middle class, and for his abrupt and blundering economic policies. Yet it also admitted that the external situation—Hungary's "encirclement" and the lack of outside support—was a major cause of the defeat.[3]

Lenin had long intended to found a new organization of Bolshevik-style parties, a centralized, disciplined movement, to replace the prewar Socialist International. The Comintern was formed in March 1919 at the very moment of victory in Hungary. Its first Congress was not very representative and was very much a Russian show. Because of the difficulty of reaching Moscow in the midst of the Russian Civil War, most of the delegates came from areas under Soviet control or just happened to be in Moscow and were not necessarily representative of any group in their home countries. The complex process of forming Communist parties was just getting underway, and some of the groups joining the Comintern in the confused years of 1919–20 were not genuinely Communist at all. Nor were the new Communist parties, as opposed to the people at the Comintern meeting, closely connected with the Soviets. Some were headed by people who were not slavish admirers of Lenin. A few Communist parties, notably those of Hungary and Austria, were created by agents sent by Moscow. Most, however, developed when the extreme left wing of the prewar Social Democratic parties broke off from their old organizations, attracted by the victory of a "socialist" revolution in Russia. In a few cases Western socialist parties decided to join the Comintern en masse; but these "Communist" parties proved to be unstable. They collapsed in a short time and had to be reformed. Unlike any other, the British Communist party was formed by the fusion of various extremist splinter groups, for whom the Labour party had never had much use. Not all the early Western Communists started off as extreme leftists; a few opportunists identified with the far right of prewar socialism saw communism as the coming thing and rushed to get in on the ground floor. More principled organizations such as the Norwegian Labor party and some anarcho-syndicalist groups, not understanding what communism was really about, affiliated with the Comintern, only to be swiftly disillusioned.[4]

In 1919 the Comintern was purely a Western organization. But by the fall of that year, Lenin had begun to fear that revolution in the West might not be imminent after all. The world revolution might not be a process of a few months or years, but a more prolonged and complex matter. The failures in Germany and Hungary, and the solidification of a belt of anticommunist regimes between Russia and the defeated Central Powers—the only Western countries that had shown any revolutionary tendencies at all—caused him to reconsider. He realized that revolution in the Western countries would be more difficult to start than one in Russia. Lenin decided that the capitalist world must be undermined by the loss of its colonies before communism could succeed there. Revolution in the "East" and the destruction of "imperialism" might have to precede revolution in the West, although Lenin was unwilling to suggest that the success of communism in the advanced countries was entirely dependent on this. (Until well after World War II, Communist theorists tended to lump all of Asia and Africa together as the "East." They assumed that all these societies were basically similar, although there was a good deal of debate about whether Japan should properly be classified with the rest.) Lenin's concern with using the Soviet position in Central Asia to influence the "East" has been described in the previous chapter.[5]

At the Comintern's Second Congress in July 1920 Lenin introduced the new "Eastern orientation." This was overshadowed by the Soviet-Polish War, which seemed to offer a last chance of early revolution in the West and the problems of tactics and organization of the Communist parties there. Unlike the First Congress, the Second Congress was a genuinely international meeting. Many of the delegates were quite ready to argue with Lenin, and many were more optimistic about early revolutions in the West than he was.

Lenin had to fight on two fronts: on one, to ensure that the Comintern's new member parties were disciplined Bolshevik-type parties under central control, clearly distinct from the Social Democrats, and, on the other, to curb left-wing extremists, who lacked the flexibility and readiness to make compromises for the long haul he now envisaged. Many Western Communists objected to the idea of participating in parliaments or unions. To counter these tendencies, which were likely to isolate the Communists and render them ineffectual sectarians, Lenin had already written his greatest essay on tactics, "Left Wing Communism, An Infantile Malady," in April-May 1920. Already implicit in the essay were the notion that the world revolution would be a lengthy process and the tactics Lenin was to introduce in the next two years. Lenin summarized his position by remarking, "The more powerful enemy can be conquered by exerting the utmost effort and by necessarily, thoroughly, carefully, attentively and skillfully taking advantage of every, even the smallest, 'rift' among the enemy, of every antagonism and interest among the bourgeoisie within the various countries, by taking advantage of every, even the smallest, opportunity of gaining a mass ally, even though the ally be temporary, vacillating, unstable, unreliable, and even conditional."[6]

At the Comintern meeting he reiterated his arguments against the left, stressing the need to work in parliaments and unions and to infiltrate government and other organizations to maintain contact with the masses. Over some opposition the Second Congress imposed on its member parties a set of 21 conditions. The most important of the conditions were designed to secure Bolshevik-style discipline and enforce a clear and absolute break between the Communists and the old Social Democrats. But the conditions were applied with a certain flexibility. For example, Lenin believed that the British Labour party's peculiar organization would allow Communists to operate successfully inside it. Instead of being ordered to break with British democratic socialism, the already distinct British Communist party was ordered to join the Labour party. However, the Labour leaders were not gullible enough to permit this. Yet the idea was not a bad one, for other people would prove less cautious.

The Second Comintern Congress decreed policy for Communist movements in Asia. Its "Theses on the National and Colonial

Question," largely based on Lenin's thinking, stressed that Asia still required a "bourgeois" revolution. The local bourgeoisie was stifled by "imperialism" and "feudalism," the latter a misleading term for local reactionaries, usually encompassing landowners and the clergy. It was thus open to an alliance with Soviet Russia and communism against the "imperialists." Local Communist parties must temporarily ally themselves with "bourgeois" "national-revolutionary" movements while maintaining their own identities. They would emphasize agrarian issues and appeal to the peasants and, once the revolution was underway, would try to achieve a quick transition to a "proletarian" revolution as in Russia.

Many Asian delegates to the Congress were not too happy about the idea of working with noncommunist nationalists. Such alliances were to prove uneasy. Cooperation was bound to be difficult, since the Communists were pledged in advance to turn against their allies, and it was difficult to decide when and how the Communists should do so—or prevent the "national-revolutionary" groups from getting in the first blow. Nevertheless, Lenin's insights that communism in Asia required alliances with "bourgeois" groups and appeals to nationalist feelings and peasant ambitions provided the basis for Soviet policy and Communist movements there. Except in China and Indonesia, however, the development of effective Communist parties in Asia proved to be a lengthy process. In India, the most important colonial country, a Communist party was not founded until 1929, although the Soviets subsidized some noncommunist extreme Indian nationalists in the interim. Between the two world wars Communists were often unable to compete successfully with nationalist groups or traditionalist ideas in the colonial world.[7]

The Second Comintern Congress had coincided with a last upsurge of hope for early revolution in Europe. It was indicative of the future that this was closely connected with the fortunes of the Red Army in the war between Poland and the Soviet state.

Since 1918 skirmishes and even full-scale battles between the Poles and the Soviets had taken place over the undefined frontier between the two. During the crucial period of the Russian Civil

War there was a de facto armistice on the Soviet-Polish front. Although not at all friendly toward the Soviets, the Polish leaders had no desire to see a White victory. They thought that a White regime would take a more uncompromising position on territorial issues than the Soviets and would be a greater threat to Poland's independence. Once the Reds had clearly defeated the Whites, the Poles resolved to launch an offensive against the Soviets designed to push the Polish frontier far to the east and, in alliance with the Ukrainian nationalist leader Petlyura, liberate the Ukraine from Soviet rule. An independent Ukraine would permanently cripple the Soviet regime's ability to advance westward.

Claiming that they were forestalling a Soviet attack, the Poles struck into the Ukraine on April 25, 1920. At first they were successful and went all the way to Kiev, taking the city on May 6. But the Poles became overextended and outran their supply line. The Red Army quickly regrouped, and the Poles got little help from the Ukrainians. The Poles had formed the unpopular aristocracy in the western Ukraine, and Petlyura's agreement to cede the Galician area to Poland as the price for Polish help discredited him. Soviet morale was high; with the Civil War nearly over, the victorious Soviet regime could now appeal to patriotic outrage at invasion by a traditional enemy of Russia. The Red Army soon threw the Poles back; in late July it neared the Bug River, the "ethnographic" frontier between purely Polish areas and the region where the Poles were a minority among Belorussians and Ukrainians. Lithuania, eager to regain its capital of Vilna, which Poland had grabbed, came in on the Soviet side. Although the Polish invasion had been an unpleasant surprise, coming at a time when the Soviet leaders had hoped for a quiet period in which to rebuild their economy, Lenin seized on the Polish defeat as an opportunity for the cause of communism. Trotsky opposed an advance into the heart of Poland on military and political grounds, maintaining that the Red Army was not strong enough to conquer Poland without an uprising by the Polish workers. Stalin and some other Soviet leaders agreed with him. The front-line commanders, however, were enthusiastic. In a rare departure from reality Lenin decided there was a good chance of a Communist uprising in Poland or at least that the prize at stake was worth a gamble. On July 30 the Soviet forces established a "Polish Revolutionary Committee" in the captured city of Bialystok; subordinate committees were established in other cities taken by the Red Army. They were intended to become the basis for a Polish Communist government.

The Western powers tried to intervene diplomatically to stop the Soviet advance. The British Foreign Secretary, Lord Curzon, proposed a cease-fire along the ethnographic frontier. After delaying on various pretexts the Soviets replied on August 9 demanding that the armistice require the Polish Army to be reduced to 50,000 men and that representatives of "workers and peasants" participate in peace talks. The families of dead Polish soldiers were to receive free land. (Since Poland still had a powerful land-owning aristocracy and land reform was a major political issue, this was a bid for political influence inside Poland.) The Soviets offered Poland a boundary even more favorable than the Curzon line. They did not reveal an additional condition communicated directly to the Poles alone; a "workers' militia" was to take over all police functions within Poland. However, the Poles rejected the armistice offer and chose to fight it out.

The "Revkom" at Bialystok was not a success, and there was no workers' uprising. Few Poles had any sympathy for communism, and none liked Russia. The Poles received military supplies from France but otherwise got little help from the Western powers.

On August 13 Mikhail Tukhachevsky's Western Front moved to outflank Warsaw from the north, a plan possibly chosen so that the Soviet forces could quickly reach the German frontier and either stir up an uprising by the German Communists or precipitate a German move against Poland. But the Soviet forces were now overstretched and outnumbered; there were only 60,000 men before Warsaw. Command jealousies helped contribute to disaster. The secondary Southwestern Front in Galicia ignored belated orders to stop its attack on Lvov and move to support Tukhachevsky. Jozef Pilsudski, the Polish commander and head of state, had carefully held back a strong reserve near Warsaw. He attacked into a nearly undefended gap in the Soviet left flank south of Warsaw. The Soviet forces were rolled up in a disastrous rout; a large number of soldiers were forced into internment in neutral East Prussia. The Poles quickly pushed the Reds east, well beyond the Bug. Lenin quickly decided to end the war; unlike his successor he did not care much about where the Soviet-Polish border ran. An armistice was concluded on October 12; the subsequent Treaty of Riga settled the Soviet boundaries in Europe until 1939. As a result Poland obtained an eastern frontier somewhat less favorable than the one it had had before April 1920.[8]

A dramatic attempt at launching a "revolution from without"—a term used occasionally in 1920 but soon discarded as too frank—had miscarried in Europe. However, the Soviets soon scored a quiet success, little noticed by the world at large, in more favorable circumstances in Outer Mongolia.

Outer Mongolia was an extremely backward country; most of its people were nomadic herdsmen ruled by a Buddhist theocracy. The Mongols had broken away from Chinese rule after the overthrow of the Manchu dynasty in 1911. But the Chinese government wished to restore its authority there, and so a Chinese force occupied the capital of Urga in 1919. There was no Communist organization in Mongolia, but in 1919 Comintern agents contacted local liberal groups. In January 1920 they encouraged the formation of the Mongolian People's party, a group of modernizing nationalists who then wished to reform, not overturn the theocratic ruler, the bogdo gegen. With the bogdo gegen's permission, some of the leaders went to Siberia to get Soviet help against the Chinese. The People's party delegation was welcomed, and the Soviets may then have decided to invade Outer Mongolia at an opportune moment. Subsequent events simplified their task. In October 1920 a White force composed of Russians, Mongols, and Japanese led by the insane Baron Ungern-Sternberg and subsidized by the Japanese government invaded Outer Mongolia to "free" it from the Chinese and establish a base for operations against Soviet Siberia. In February 1921 this force captured Urga. Ungern-Sternberg treated the bogdo gegen as a puppet. His crazed actions alienated everyone and provided a convenient justification for Soviet intervention. The Soviets could honestly claim to be moving into Outer Mongolia in self-defense to avoid a conflict with the Chinese, whose authority Ungern-Sternberg had already overthrown.

In March the Soviets helped their Mongolian friends form a "Mongolian People's Provisional Government" in exile in Siberia. There was nothing overtly Communist about this organization, which was pledged to implement a very modest program of reforms (e.g., the abolition of slavery). A small Mongol armed force was also formed. The force captured a small area of Outer Mongolia, where the Provisional Government joined it and issued a request for Soviet help. As Soviet diplomats blandly assured the Chinese government that they had no intention of attacking Outer Mongolia, the Red Army moved in and crushed Ungern-Sternberg's forces. When the Provisional Government arrived in Urga, it was reorganized on a broader basis. The bogdo gegen remained the nominal head of state until his death in 1924. The regime was kept under close Soviet supervision while growing numbers of Mongol Communists were trained. The Soviets politely informed the Chinese that they had better not interfere. In 1922 most of the original members of the Provisional Government were shot. After the death of the bogdo gegen, Outer Mongolia became a "People's Republic." By stages over a period of many years, it was transformed into a reliable satellite state ruled by an orthodox, Soviet-style Communist party. Along with various operations within the boundaries of the old Russian empire, Outer Mongolia was a proving ground for methods that were used successfully on a much larger scale in Eastern Europe and North Korea after World War II.[9] Despite its failure in Poland, the Red Army was to be a very much more effective instrument of revolution than the efforts of foreign Communist parties.

The conquest of Outer Mongolia, however, was an exceptional episode at that time. Soviet operations in Asia were largely confined to nursing the formation of Communist parties and forming alliances with existing regimes aimed at "imperialism," and especially against the British. The Soviet government had renounced the Imperial government's special privileges and concessions in such "semicolonial" countries as China and Iran, paving the way for such alliances. In the spring of 1920 the Soviets did make an abortive move into Iran, which was badly disorganized. Chasing remnants of Denikin's forces, the Red Army entered the province of Gilan. There the Soviets supported Kuchik Khan, a local revolutionary and a fierce enemy of the British; although not a Communist, he proclaimed a "Soviet Republic of Gilan." But the Soviets decided that they were too weak to take Iran in the face of a probable British reaction and therefore came to terms with the non-Communist Iranians. They made an alliance with Reza Khan, a general who was more conservative than Kuchik Khan but was then anti-British. (Reza Khan later proclaimed himself shah and founded the short-lived Pahlevi dynasty that was overthrown in 1979.) The Soviets followed similar policies toward the reforming king of Afghanistan. In Turkey the Soviets formed an alliance with Kemal Ataturk, a reforming nationalist who had revolted against the sultan and was struggling against the Allied occupation forces and the Greeks. In the first instance of Soviet aid to a non-Communist country, Kemal received Soviet weapons, but he was careful to avoid the growth of Soviet influence. He tolerated the growth of a "national Communist" group, the "Green Apple," whose ideas were rather far removed from those of Lenin. But the orthodox, Soviet-oriented Turkish Communist party was ruthlessly crushed.

Lenin glumly turned a blind eye to this. Although not a serious reverse from his point of view, for the Turkish Communists were not a serious force nor likely to become one, this episode pointed to a serious dilemma for Soviet policies in the future. Aid to or an alliance with a local government or a "bourgeois" national movement aimed against the "imperialists" always posed the danger that the non-Communist "client" might turn against the local Communists; in fact Soviet aid might strengthen the non-Communists against Moscow's own followers. Moreover, there was no real escape from this dilemma. Some critics who liked to imagine themselves better revolutionaries than the Soviets or felt that the interests of communism in underdeveloped countries were being sacrificed to the perhaps misconceived interests of the Soviet state criticized the whole idea of working with non-Communist regimes or movements. The rejection of such alliances, however, was not a practical option for the Soviets. A refusal to work with men like Ataturk or Reza Shah posed the danger that countries such as Turkey and Iran, adjacent to Soviet territory, might come under direct Western control or powerful influence, which was obviously not acceptable. A policy of limiting Soviet support to Communist movements only and stipulating complete freedom of action for the local Communists throughout was likely to drive non-Communist nationalists into the arms of the West or at least inspire them to take a firmly anticommunist stand from the first. In fact, a stage of friendly relations between Communists and "bourgeois" nationalists seems to have been necessary for the former to develop effective mass movements in Asia and Africa. The problem of when to terminate such alliances or recognize that an ally was about to turn on the Communists proved extremely difficult. It could not be planned in advance, and Moscow found it difficult to manage such situations intelligently by remote control.[10] Nor was the dilemma to disappear with the passage of time. In practice Soviet policies in backward countries have tended to alternate between periods of emphasis on the local Communists and the overthrow of the local regimes, as for example in the last part of the Stalin era, and periods when the stress has been on alliances with non-Communists against the West, as in the Khrushchev era. Neither line of policy has ever entirely disappeared.

Obnoxious from the standpoint of the British, the Soviet establishment of friendly relations with neighboring "nationalist" regimes coincided with a normalization of diplomatic relations and trade between the Soviets and the Western countries, although relations between the Western democracies and the Soviets remained poor throughout the period preceding the rise of Nazism in Germany. The years 1919–20, and what has been aptly called the "Red Mirage" of an early world revolution, saw a feverish "Red

Scare" in much of the Western world, although the emotions it expressed often had little to do with the rise of Communist totalitarianism, stemming instead from hatred of the labor movement and even murkier motives. Like McCarthyism in the early 1950s the Red Scare was at best only tangentially related and perhaps opposed to the efforts of genuine anti-Communists like Churchill. After the last Western forces had left Russia in 1920, the Western powers did remarkably little to counter effectively the Soviet regime and the world Communist movement. Except for a brief period in 1919, Russia had never really been the focus of attention for Western foreign relations; that honor went to the German problem. Only the episode of the Hungarian Soviet Republic had frightened the Western leaders into taking the threat of world revolution seriously for a short time.

Nonetheless, moral disapproval of the Soviet regime, rather than fear of it, remained widespread. The United States and many of the smaller European countries refrained from establishing diplomatic relations with the Soviet government, although they traded freely with the Soviets and the Americans had extended vital famine relief. The reasoning behind U.S. policy was explained by Secretary of State Colby in 1920. Colby remarked that the "existing regime in Russia is based upon the negation of every principle upon which it is possible to base harmonious and trustful relations, whether of nations or individuals," citing the Soviet policy of promoting revolution.[11]

The British and the other great powers followed a pragmatic policy. The Soviet government was there and had to be dealt with. Diplomatic relations might be deplorable, but they were necessary. But the British found their policy difficult to follow consistently. Issues of Russian debts repudiated by the Soviets and outrage at Soviet propaganda and efforts to interfere in British colonies and Britain herself, which were sometimes magnified and manipulated by elements of the Conservative party, made it difficult to go beyond the state of de facto relations established in 1921. In a famous episode in 1924 the Conservatives made use of a forged letter attributed to Grigori Zinoviev, the head of the Comintern, to embarrass the Labour party. When the British police raided the offices of a Soviet trade mission in May 1927, they uncovered much evidence of actual Soviet espionage and secret activities designed to promote the British Communist party. This led to a complete break in relations until 1930, when Britain and the Soviet Union finally exchanged ambassadors.

Britain and France remained the main enemies for the Soviet leaders. Their inability to compose their differences with the Germans enabled the Soviets to form a limited sort of alliance in 1922 with the Weimar Republic. This Treaty of Rapallo was followed by important secret agreements on military matters. Arrangements were made that helped the Germans to evade the disarmament clauses of the Treaty of Versailles by allowing the development of equipment and training for air and tank forces on Soviet territory. In return the Germans helped modernize the Red Army; Soviet officers, including the future Marshal Georgi Zhukov, received training in Germany. A strange dual relationship developed between the two states similar to that between the Soviets and the nationalist regimes in underdeveloped countries; for while cultivating the German government as an ally against the major Western powers, the Soviets continued to plot its overthrow by the German Communists. Despite much anger and alarm in the West, the Soviet-German tie remained short of a true military alliance because the Weimar leaders placed primary emphasis on improving relations with Britain and France. The link with the Soviets was partly a means of encouraging the Allied countries to take a friendlier view of Germany.[12]

The early 1920s saw the beginning of a small-scale secret war between Soviet and Western intelligence agencies. In a rather feeble riposte for the flood of Soviet agents appearing in the West, the British and French intelligence agencies aided Russian emigré groups, mainly monarchists, who tried to penetrate the Soviet Union with agents and contact underground opposition forces there, occasionally committing terrorist acts against Soviet officials. The monarchists proved a poor choice. Very conservative Western officials may have preferred them to leftist emigrés on political grounds, but unlike the left they had few links with the Soviet official class. (By contrast, a remarkable proportion of Soviet officials and technicians were former Mensheviks.) And the Soviets found the monarchists easy prey. In 1922 Soviet intelligence skillfully launched an operation of their own, the "Trust," and penetrated the monarchist emigré groups. The Soviets gained much control over their operations inside the U.S.S.R. and were able to gain much information on Western activities in general. The Poles, who at first were also taken in by the Trust, were rather more successful in their independent operations against the Soviets. One amazing Polish agent, Konar, assuming a dead man's identity, operated in Soviet territory for a decade, rising to become assistant commissar of agriculture before he was exposed by an accident.

After it became clear that the Russian monarchist groups were of little value, the British and other intelligence agencies for a time subsidized a new emigré organization, the Narodny Truboe Soyuz (literally "People's Labor Alliance") founded in 1930. Originally democratic in orientation, the organization tended to drift toward Italian-style fascism during the 1930s, though later moving back to the moderate right. Unlike other emigré groups, it seems to have had some success at getting agents and propaganda into the Soviet Union, but there is little sign that it really achieved much for itself or its patrons. As a string of costly failures in the late 1940s and early 1950s showed, the Soviet state was almost impossible to penetrate from the outside, even for emigrés; as far as is known, all Western espionage successes in the post–World War II era have been due to the recruitment of "defectors-in place."[13]

On the whole, Western intelligence accomplished little of value in its offensive operations. In contrast, defensive operations, aided by Soviet defectors, were sometimes very successful. When former secretary to the Politburo Boris Bajanov defected in 1928, he exposed and ruined a Soviet plan to seize control of Iran with the help of a network of agents reaching as high as the shah's court. In 1931 the British police in Singapore arrested a French Comintern agent, Ducroux; this led to the capture of a number of Communist leaders in China and Southeast Asia, including the then obscure figure of Nguyen Ai Quoc—better known as Ho Chi Minh—and some records of Comintern's Far Eastern Bureau. In general, during the years between the world wars Communist organizations in the British, Dutch, and French colonies were promptly suppressed when uncovered, although the Dutch and the French hardly treated noncommunist nationalists any better.[14]

The Western powers failed to use what might well have been the most effective countermeasure against the Soviet Union: economic warfare. They made no effort to stop or even discourage trade with the Soviet Union, which received capital goods and strategic materials throughout Stalin's industrialization drive. Indeed, during the 1930s Soviet industrialization was greatly aided by Western engineers and skilled workers. Factories were constructed in the Soviet Union by great Western industrial concerns such as Ford, General Electric, and RCA.

During 1921 the Comintern decided on "long-haul" policies. An abortive uprising in Germany in March 1921 instigated by a faction in the Comintern in Moscow without regard for Lenin's views made it clear that the revolutionary wave in Europe, such as it was, had spent itself. The Comintern's Third Congress admitted that a relative stabilization of capitalism had occurred. Policies had to change. Communists must maintain contact with the "masses" and establish alliances designed to utilize non-Communist strength. Having clearly broken with Social Democratic parties and established their own identity, Communist parties in the Western world were ordered to establish "united fronts" or alliances with Social Democrats. In a related vein the Comintern began to promote the development and use of groups and organizations apparently unconnected with the Communists but effectively controlled by them. An ingenious German Communist, Willi Muenzenberg, was a particularly able organizer of what he sardonically referred to as "Innocents' Clubs." Later Communists preferred to call them "transmission belts," "satellite organizations," or "peripheral organizations," but they are better known as "front organizations," though Communists themselves do not use this term. "Front" in Communist parlance is short for "united front." But it should be remembered that the ideal outcome of a united front is to turn the organization or alliance thus created into front organizations in the non-Communist sense. And front organizations often pose as alliances; a classic example was the National Liberation Front of South Vietnam. Such front organizations might not necessarily be created by Communists; they might be originally independent groups infiltrated by them and then taken over. Some fronts acted as substitutes for the Communist party itself, for their purported aim coincided with the party's minimum program or some part of it. They were valuable as a means of marshaling and directing sympathizers with communism who lacked the courage to join the party, and for providing access to sectors of society where overt Communists could not move. Other fronts could be used to organize and absorb non-Communist leftists or were designed to use non-Communists, even anticommunists, to support a single issue on which they happened to agree with the Communists. Neither the "united front" concept nor the "front organization" was a complete departure from previous practices. Both represented logical extensions of previous Leninist tactics and had precedents in the Russian events of 1917–18. The coalition with the Left Socialist Revolutionaries was the first united front, and the Soviets had been transformed into the first front organizations. Both devices showed that the Communists realized that their creed was not, generally speaking, especially popular, and that it was often more effective to act in the name of some other organization or cause than in the name of the party itself. The concept "united front," in particular, expressed the Communists' stress on the problem of alliances—how to secure them, how to make use of them, and when to turn against one's partner.[15]

The developments of 1921 reflected the last major turn in Soviet and Comintern policy introduced by Lenin, who was in poor health and played a rapidly diminishing role in affairs. Lenin now estimated that a considerable period would pass before the final global victory. In 1921 he rather vaguely suggested that "victory on a world scale" might be assured in as little as ten years, if things went well. Otherwise, it might take as long as 40 years. In his last published work, "Better Fewer But Better" (March 1923), Lenin reiterated the emphasis on the East and long-haul policies developed in 1919–21. Pessimistic about the near future, he warned not to rely on the idea that "we possess any considerable quantity of the elements necessary for building a really new apparatus that would really deserve the name of socialist, Soviet, and so forth." But in long-term aims he had not softened one bit. "Russia, India, China, and others, contain the vast majority of the world's people. This majority has driven itself ever faster in the last years into the war for its freedom, and in this sense there can be no shadow of a doubt as to the eventual decision in the world struggle. In this sense the final victory of socialism is fully and unconditionally guaranteed. ... In order to secure (our) existence until the final military conflict between the counter-revolutionary imperialist West and the revolutionary and nationalist East, between the civilized states of the world and the Eastern remainder, which however, comprises the majority—it is necessary to succeed in civilizing this majority."[16]

A last set of failures in Europe proved once more that Lenin's appreciation had been correct. The year 1923 saw the development of an apparently promising crisis in Germany. The conflict over war reparations led to the occupation of the Ruhr by French and Belgian forces; passive resistance by the German government led to hyperinflation, economic collapse, enormous unemployment, and waves of strikes. All this was misread by Moscow as indicating the development of a revolutionary situation. On August 23 the Soviet Politburo resolved to launch a revolution in Germany. A plan was laid for an uprising centered in Saxony and Thuringia. These states were ruled by left-wing Social Democrats who had been cooperating with the Communists—this was one of the few successes achieved by the united front policy. The local Communists were to join the governments of those states, which had very bad relations with the conservative government in Berlin, and organize an uprising using left-wing socialist support and local institutions as a cover. Unlike previous revolutionary attempts in Europe, this effort would receive direct Soviet aid and be closely supervised by Soviet "civil war experts." These men, along with weapons, were smuggled into Germany. Preparations were made for a "German October Revolution." But the Communists had been hypnotized by the development of the German Communist party's strength, for its membership and support had grown considerably, and they had failed to take a realistic view of other factors. There was no evidence that a majority of the workers supported the Communists. Neither Chancellor Stresemann nor the Social Democratic leaders were Kerenskys; the Communists misjudged even their political allies among the Left Social Democrats. Their armed strength was far inferior to that of the army, which was a strongly anticommunist all-volunteer force. Moreover, the Communist growth in strength was more than counterbalanced by that of the far right, which had armed units of its own.

The Communists had barely joined the Saxon and Thuringian governments when the central government, well aware of their preparations, took counteraction. On October 13 the government began moving troops into those states and took control of the police there. The Communists called for a general strike to protest "repression"; this was to be a prelude to an uprising. However, their Social Democratic "allies" would not act. Suddenly realizing their actual weakness, the Communists canceled the revolt; but by mistake their Hamburg section failed to get the message—or perhaps just ignored it. An isolated uprising there was quickly crushed. An uprising in Bulgaria was also defeated, and a planned revolt in Finland simply fizzled.[17] As Lenin's rule came to an end, it became clear that the Soviet Union would be thrown on its own resources for an indefinite period.

Stalinism

The struggle for Lenin's succession was won by the Georgian Bolshevik Josef Djugashvili, better known by his party name of Stalin. As the ruler of the Soviet Union for nearly three decades, Stalin placed a brutal imprint of his own on the Soviet Union, the world Communist movement, and much of the world. In some respects he carried many of the tendencies in Lenin's thought to an extreme, heightening its already considerable bent toward tyranny and militarism. The Soviet Union became an industrialized "superpower," helped to win World War II, conquered half of Europe, and came very close to starting a third world war. Stalin in fact decided in 1951 to launch such a war, which was averted only by his death in March 1953.[1]

Stalin had not been in the first rank of the Communist party leadership before the revolution. He had distinguished himself by his ability to gain funds for the Bolsheviks by criminal methods and for his unwavering loyalty to Lenin, who was perhaps the only human being he truly admired. Stalin was commissar of nationalities in the Soviet government from its foundation, and he occupied other important posts. In 1918 he supervised the defense of Tsaritsyn—later renamed after him—against the Cossacks. Although Stalin was poorly educated and his colleagues looked down on him, he was a capable administrator and a master of intrigue. Unlike the unassuming Lenin, Stalin was basically arrogant and nasty. Yet he could put on a mask of charm, and this proved useful in dealing with foreigners. A patient and careful man, at least until the last years of his life, he excelled in weaving fantastically complex and deadly plots that took years to complete. An old Bolshevik, F. F. Raskolnikov, write of Stalin that "in the silence of his office, in deep solitude, he carefully figures out a plan of action and with fine calculation strikes sudden and true." He noted that "No one can compete with Stalin in the art of tricking."[2] By accepting the dull, and apparently unrewarding administrative post of secretary-general of the party's Central Committee, he gained control of the party's organizational machinery, and finally of its policy-making machinery as well.

Stalin had spent little time outside the Russian empire, and unlike Lenin and many other old Bolsheviks, he was not very well informed about the outside world. He tended to project Russian conditions onto other countries to a greater extent than his predecessor. But Stalin was extremely clever at exploiting the weaknesses and conflicts of others, and he was adept at playing off his enemies, foreign and domestic, against each other. He specialized in making agents of people who had dubious political pasts and were entirely dependent on his protection. A notable example of this was the former Menshevik Andrei Vyshinsky, who became the prosecutor in the purge trial of the 1930s and rose to become Stalin's last foreign minister in 1949. After World War II Stalin made use of individuals who had been pro-German or had even been outright fascists, such as the Romanian politician Gheorghe Tatarescu and the Polish fascist leader Boleslaw Piasecki. They assisted him in the takeover of some Eastern European countries.

Unlike Adolf Hitler, Stalin knew where to stop, at least until 1951. But he was a man of insatiable vanity, an unquenchable thirst for power, and growing paranoid fears. In external affairs this meant he was never really satisfied with just an ordinary alliance or even mere submission. His behavior in the 1940s reduced the Czech foreign minister, Jan Masaryk, to groaning, "You can be on your knees, and it's not enough for the Russians!" Even the allegiance of a "fellow Communist" was not good enough; men like Tito and Mao Zedong (Mao Tse-tung), though successful and deferential to Stalin, had to be destroyed and replaced by mere puppets. Even in the countries where the Communist rulers were installed by the Red Army, Stalin insisted on bypassing or purging leaders of local origin in favor of men like Matyas Rakosi and Kim Il Sung, who had been exiles in the Soviet Union.

Stalin was so selfish and so brutally cynical that it has reasonably been asked whether he was ever actuated by a belief in communism at all. He was certainly unable to subordinate his personal power interests to the interests of the Soviet state or the world Communist movement. But he was not merely a power-obsessed cynic, for he really believed the system he built was "socialism" and constituted something incomparably superior to anything else in the world. The Yugoslav Communist Milovan Djilas, who observed him closely in the 1940s, remarked of Stalin: "He was one of those rare terrible dogmatists capable of destroying nine tenths of the human race to make happy the one tenth," and "all in all, Stalin was a monster, who, while adhering to abstract, absolute and fundamentally utopian ideas, in practice recognized, and could only recognize, only success—violence, and physical and spiritual extermination."[3] Even Khrushchev's two volumes of memoirs, though bitterly critical of Stalin, do not question Stalin's loyalty to communism. Indeed, some of Stalin's worst mistakes seem to have stemmed from the fact that he saw the world through a Marxist-Leninist prism. It was ideology, not just political machinations, that saddled a disastrously unproductive system of state and collective farms on the Soviet Union. As Conrad Brandt has shown, the failure of the attempt to launch a Communist revolution in China in the 1920s (discussed in the next chapter) was due partly to the inability to see that China did not quite fit the Leninist stereotype. According to Khrushchev, after 1949 he rationalized his hostility to Mao on "Marxist" grounds, grumbling that Mao was not a "true" Communist because the Chinese leader had admitted that he had deliberately delayed the capture of Shanghai, since the workers there did not support communism.

Overcoming Lenin's last-minute misgivings about him and using his own base of power in the party machinery, Stalin gradually defeated a whole series of opponents. First with the help of Lev Kamenev and Grigori Zinoviev he beat Trotsky, his most formidable rival for Lenin's succession. Then he combined with Nikolai Bukharin and Aleksei Rykov, "rightists" of moderate temper, against the "leftists" Kamenev and Zinoviev. Then adopting the program of the very "leftists" he had just beaten, he overcame Bukharin and Rykov. Stalin's method of dealing with his Soviet rivals has been aptly described by Robert Conquest: "Stalin would attack and discredit a man, then appear to reach a compromise, leaving his opponent weakened but not destroyed. Bit by bit their positions were undermined, and they were removed one by one from the leadership."[4] Similar step-by-step techniques appear in his handling of foreign affairs.

Terminating the New Economic Policy in 1928, Stalin launched a veritable second revolution. He began a ruthless program of forced collectivization of the peasantry, forced settlement of nomadic peoples, and a crash program of industrialization. Collectivization led to the slaughter of *kulaks* (rich peasants) and to a gigantic artificial famine in the Ukraine, Kazakhstan, and the Volga region. The destruction of the most efficient farmers, the slaughter of animals by the remaining peasants, and the imposition of a system basically unsuitable for farming would permanently hobble Soviet agriculture. But Stalin got what he wanted: The peasants and some of the non-Russian nationalities were brought to heel, and the maximum surplus extracted to help pay for industrialization. Later, in the Great Purges, Stalin destroyed most of the original Communist party, including his own supporters, rebuilding it as his personal instrument.[5]

In relations with foreign countries and in directing foreign Communists, Stalin was initially cautious about altering Lenin's policies; he may at first have been too preoccupied to do so.

During the struggle for succession Stalin tried to develop a reputation as a theoretician, something he had previously lacked. In fact his views were not very original. They were mostly restatements or short-range extrapolations of views earlier expressed by Lenin. His views on the external relations of the Soviet Union and the policies the Comintern should follow were closely related to the policy of "building socialism in one country," Stalin's solution to the theoretical impasse in which the Russian Communists had been left by the failure of revolution in the West.

Stalin maintained that the Soviet Union could build "socialism," that is, a society that had reached the "socialist" stage of Marx's schema, within its own boundaries and without assistance from a more advanced "socialist" country in the West. However, the Soviet Union would not be safe from attack, and the victory of socialism would not be "final and complete" until revolutions had occurred in a "number of countries." Lenin had moved toward this position in his last years, though without great enthusiasm. Trotsky clearly opposed this notion, maintaining that the Soviets could begin the process of "building socialism" but could not finish it without revolution in the West. R. N. Carew-Hunt has neatly summarized the position of the two sides in this controversy: "In the Stalinist scheme the establishment of socialism in Russia came first and world revolution second; in the Trotskyist conception this order was reversed." It is by no means the case that, as is sometimes claimed, Stalin rejected "world revolution" in favor of "socialism in one country," and this idea was in fact stigmatized as a stupid deviation in the Soviet Union.

"Socialism in one country" implied a greater role for the Soviet state as the "base" for carrying on the world revolution, which lost any remaining connotation of being a quick chain reaction of basically internal upheavals.[6] Rather, in the Stalin era and after it was envisaged as a "more or less lengthy process of Communist conquest encompassing many diverse revolutionary currents," as Kermit McKenzie has put it.[7] In fact, the idea of world revolution became close to, though perhaps not quite identical with, the concept of a Soviet conquest of the whole world. For Stalin was quite pessimistic about the spread of revolution in Western countries in the near future.

In analyzing the Russian revolution Stalin especially stressed that the main enemy of the revolution had been "petty-bourgeois democrats." Even more than Lenin, Stalin hated liberals and democratic socialists more than the extreme right. He consistently seemed to prefer to have Communists ally themselves with reactionaries and fascists. It cannot be too strongly emphasized that the Communist movement was fundamentally oriented toward a struggle with "bourgeois democracy," not fascism. (Fascism, after all, had not existed when Lenin formulated his ideas.) Especially for Stalin, the need to fight fascism was a highly unwelcome interruption of the fight against what had always been regarded as the main enemy.

Stalin stressed the importance of favorable external conditions, primarily arising from the world war, which had led to the revolution and had distracted the "imperialist powers." The lack of a Communist-ruled state elsewhere was the only unfavorable external condition facing the Bolsheviks. The support of the workers, poor peasants, and soldiers, the weakness of the Russian bourgeoisie, the agrarian problem, and Russia's size and resources, which had enabled the revolution to survive blockade, had constituted the internal conditions favorable to the revolution. None of these conditions existed to any extent in any Western country except Spain, which did have an agrarian problem similar to Russia's. Stalin cited Lenin's remark that "it will be more difficult for Western Europe to *start* a socialist revolution than it was for us." However, many of the conditions favorable to revolution existed in Asia. Indeed, in his major theoretical work, *Foundations of Leninism* (actually largely cribbed from a man named Ksenofontov, whom Stalin later had purged), Stalin stressed the necessity of attacking capitalism where the "chain of imperialism" was weakest, in Asia. He also alluded to the use of armed Soviet intervention; in several of his writings he cited Lenin's 1915 remarks about "coming out even with armed force against the exploiting classes and their states." According to the Indian Communist M. N. Roy, Stalin remarked in 1925 that no revolution could succeed in Europe unless the Red Army brought it there; "now it is our task to build up an army and defeat the combined might of the capitalist world."[8] In January 1925 Stalin told a meeting of the Central

Committee, "If war breaks out we shall not be able to sit with folded arms. We shall have to take action, but we shall be the last to do so. And we shall do so in order to throw the decisive weight on the scales, the weight that will tip the balance."[9]

Under Stalin's rule the Comintern's importance dwindled. Whatever independence it had ever had vanished completely, and it became just a tool of the Soviet state. Its congresses, which were nominally supposed to occur every year, became rare events. Its Sixth Congress, held in 1928, did complete the Stalinization of the world Communist movement. That movement now began to suffer its first permanent split as the followers of Trotsky, who was exiled from the Soviet Union in 1929, began to establish their own movement. Although the Trotskyites were not very effective, the existence of a "Communist" opposition enraged Stalin. His agents fought them all over the world and finally hunted Trotsky down in Mexico in 1940, killing him.

The Sixth Comintern Congress announced that the period of the "stabilization of capitalism" was coming to an end. It stressed that the "international character" of the class struggle was growing; it forecast a period of wars in the relatively near future and emphasized the duty of Communists in other countries to support the Red Army. Harping on the theme that war was the road to revolution, it claimed that any wars would be started by the "imperialists." However, it carefully hinted that the real issue was not who was the aggressor but who represented "reaction." The Comintern stressed the need for "revolutionary defeatist" activities by Western Communists in the event of war. The Sixth Congress cautiously expressed the Communists' growing de-emphasis on the "proletariat" as the key revolutionary class, and it recognized openly that other groups, notably peasants in underdeveloped countries, had far greater revolutionary potential. It stressed that the colonies were the most vulnerable point of the "imperialist front." In short-term tactics the Sixth Congress continued the rejection of the "united front from above," abandoned in 1924. After 1924, while rejecting alliances with Social Democratic parties, the Communists had agitated for a "united front from below." This was merely an appeal to the Social Democratic rank and file to abandon their leaders. But the Social Democrats were not just unsuitable as allies. They were now seen as the main enemy, the principal prop of "bourgeois democracy." The destruction of democratic socialism now became the main aim of the Communist parties in the West.

On the whole, however, Stalin apparently did not expect real results from Communist activities abroad in 1928. The thunder of the Sixth Comintern Congress was probably due largely to Stalin's feeling that an atmosphere of crisis was desirable as a background for collectivization and the industrialization drive. Thus the arrival of the Great Depression came as a pleasant surprise.[10] But neither the Soviet Union nor its followers abroad were in a very good position to accomplish much. In fact, they had suffered a major reverse in Stalin's first effort at expansion, which was also the first effort at achieving a Communist revolution in a major Asian country.

The Struggle for China, 1924–1935

The attempt to stage a Communist takeover in China was the first serious effort to carry out the policy for Asia outlined by the Second Comintern Congress. It was also Stalin's first major move in foreign affairs. Although soon taking on a dynamism of its own, the Chinese Communist movement originated as a Soviet effort to outflank the West.

As Lenin had foreseen, over the next several decades the most effective appeals of Communist parties in East Asia exploited the issues of nationalism and land tenure. Nationalism as an organizing basis took different forms in the various countries and was made available to the Communists only by Japanese invasion, by exceptionally stubborn colonial regimes, or a combination of the two. The land issue, though less effective than national survival or independence as a basis of appeal, was a steadier and more dependable source of discontent. Despite vast differences in political structure and degree of industrialization, a strikingly similar situation existed in the rural areas of all the East Asian nations from Japan to Vietnam. It formed the social background of the political conflicts of the region until the belated South Vietnamese land reform in 1970. The majority of peasants were tenants who owned little or none of the pocket-sized slices of land that they worked. Paying heavy rents, they were always in debt and had no security of tenure or enforceable contracts with their landlords. The latter performed no economic function; "improving landlords" were unknown in Asia outside Japan. The discontent of the peasants was exploited by right-wing fanatics in Japan and by Communists in other countries until the situation was ended in the quarter century after World War II by reform in Japan, Korea, Taiwan, and South Vietnam, and by revolution in China and North Vietnam. Despite Lenin's injunction, the Communists took a long time to realize fully the importance of the land question and to get into position to exploit it. In China and Indonesia, the only countries where parties of significant strength developed in the 1920s, the Communists at first concentrated on building their strength in urban, not rural, areas. In fact, some major external crisis or disruption of the local political system was necessary to break the inertia of the populace and make it possible to contact the peasants and mobilize them.

The Soviets would very much have preferred to see a revolutionary movement in Japan rather than China. But the Japanese Communist party developed very slowly. It was repeatedly smashed by the police and failed to develop much influence.

China was a much better target. It had been reduced to a state of chaos by the overthrow of the Manchu dynasty in 1911 and the failure of its republican successors to form a stable regime. China was divided among an unstable, shifting group of provincial army leaders, the "warlords," who constantly fought among themselves. The Western powers and the Japanese, who held extensive "concessions" and settlements in China's coastal and river ports, and in some cases broader spheres of influence, recognized whoever held the old imperial capital of Beijing (Peking) as the nominal government of China. The outside powers had introduced some modern industry into China, but their encroachments had weakened the Chinese government and inflamed Chinese nationalism without imposing any positive order of their own. Albeit somewhat exaggerating the impact of the West on the situation in China, the remark of a British writer that "it was nihilist exploitation by 'old China hands' and not direct rule by 'Indian Civilians' (i.e. the

renowned Indian Civil Service) which evoked a Soviet substitute"
contains some truth.[1] Some elements of China's traditional culture
and social order helped pave the way for the acceptance of Communist doctrine. Religion did not form a barrier to the spread of
communism, as it tended to do in the Islamic world and India.
Some Confucian beliefs and the traditional deference to the rule of
the mandarinate, the scholar-gentry, were readily transformed into
support for the Communist party. Though not large, the Chinese
working class was severely exploited. Child labor and a twelve-
hour day were common.[2]

The Soviet government's renunciation of Russia's special privileges in China in 1919 had attracted some enthusiasm in China,
which was strongly at odds with the Western powers and Japan.
Japan's attempt to gain control of China during World War I was
much resented, as was the West's agreement to Japan's retention
of the German possessions in China captured during the war. The
Russian Revolution caused Chinese intellectuals to become very
interested in "Marxism," which in China was seen through a
Leninist prism. During 1920–21 Comintern agents helped fuse
Marxist study groups into the Chinese Communist party, formally
founded in Shanghai in July 1921. At first it included wayward
democratic socialists and anarchists; these gradually dropped out
or were eliminated.

The Soviets searched for some existing source of power or
nationalist movement with which to ally themselves. For a time
they tried to cultivate the central government and various northern
warlords, but without much success. It became apparent that no
base of operations in China could be secured in any area near the
Soviet-Chinese frontier.

Comintern agents had more success in South China. There they
contacted Sun l-xian (Sun Yat-sen), the head of the Guomintang
(Kuomintang), or Nationalist party, and the founder of the Chinese
Republic. Chased out of Beijing, he had taken refuge in the south
and for a time was uneasily allied with a reformist local warlord.
Sun's program called for freeing China from outside encroachments, forming a democratic republic after a period of "tutelage"

under the rule of the Guomindang, land reform, and nationalization of basic industries. He was no Marxist but had long felt friendly toward the Bolsheviks, and his party desperately needed aid and organization. After unsuccessfully seeking help from other countries, especially the United States, he was amenable to an alliance with the Soviets, which was reached in January 1923. The Soviets professed to accept the Guomindang's claim to lead the Chinese revolution, feeding Sun a somewhat twisted version of Communist doctrine to assure him that they did not envisage a Communist revolution in China in the near future. The Nationalists' alliance with the Soviet Union was to be paralleled by an alliance with the Chinese Communist party. The Soviets pressured the reluctant Chinese Communist leaders into agreeing to an alliance with Sun, whom they disliked. Sun would not agree to a simple two-party alliance, so a special device, the "bloc within," was introduced. It was agreed that some members of the Chinese Communist party would join the Guomindang as individuals, but the Communist party retained a separate existence. The Soviets justified this by the claim, which they apparently believed, that the Guomindang was not really a single political party but a multiclass alliance including the "bourgeoisie" and the peasantry. A large mission of Soviet political and military advisers under Mikhail Borodin arrived in Canton in September 1923. They reorganized the Guomindang on centralized Leninist principles and helped found a military academy. They organized and armed the Nationalist armed forces. Meanwhile, the Chinese Communists entered the Guomindang, assuming key posts in its organizational, propaganda, labor, and peasant affairs departments. Outside Canton itself the Communists dominated the growing labor movement.

The Soviets promoted the rise of Jiang Jieshi (Chiang Kai-Shek), one of Sun's lieutenants, and helped place him in charge of the Nationalist armed forces. Jiang was at first friendly to the Soviets and had been associated with the most pro-Soviet Guomindang leaders. But a trip to Moscow in 1923–24 caused him to become disillusioned with the Soviet regime. He became the leader of the Guomindang's "centrist" faction, which favored maintaining the alliance with the Soviets and the Chinese Communists, but he had greater reservations about them than about the Guomindang left, led by Wang Jingwei (Wang Ching-wei). The Communists allied themselves with the left and played the left and center off against the anti-Communist right, which after Sun's death in 1925 had come to favor breaking with the Soviets. The left triumphed and Wang became the head of the government in August, 1925. That year experienced a sharp upsurge in nationalist feeling and labor unrest throughout southern and central China. The Communists were still concentrating on the labor movement. The Chinese were enraged when British and French police and troops killed demonstrators in Shanghai and Canton and were unappeased by the knowledge that their own warlords did such things. The Guomindang prepared for a major military campaign, the "Northern Expedition," against the warlords. Unenthusiastic about an early move of this sort, the Communists preferred to gain control of the Guomindang-Communist base area in South China before embarking on territorial expansion.

Jiang Jieshi, however, had decided to curb the Soviets and the Chinese Communists before moving north. Thus on March 20, 1926, claiming that he was acting to forestall a Communist plot to kidnap him while Borodin was away, Jiang arrested a number of Communist leaders, disarmed a Communist-led "workers' militia," and confined the Soviet advisors to their quarters. Having assumed that the Nationalists were entirely dependent on them for arms, the Soviets were taken by surprise. But Jiang did not want a complete break with either the Soviets or the Chinese Communists, although the latter, supported by some Comintern agents, were now eager to escape the embrace of the Guomindang. The Soviets agreed to a settlement on Jiang's terms. Their advisors would be deprived of the power of command, while the Chinese Communists would be removed from leading positions in the Guomindang and the number of Communists in decision-making positions at lower levels would be limited, as was the Communists' freedom of action to agitate among the peasants.

Wang Jingwei was forced from office; in June 1926 Jiang became chairman of the Guomindang. After defeating a preemptive offensive by the supreme northern warlord, Wu Peifu, the Nationalists launched the Northern Expedition in July 1926. Masterful propaganda and organization by the Guomindang and the Communists made the offensive an unexpectedly easy triumph. The warlord forces fled, collapsed, or came over to the Nationalists. Although some ugly incidents occurred during the Northern Expedition, the foreign powers began to come to terms with Chinese nationalism, and they offered to negotiate about the concessions with the Nationalist government.

During the march north the Communists regained some of their freedom of action and were highly successful at organizing peasants and labor in the newly won areas. They seemed to recoup much of what had been lost in March 1926. The Soviets had also formed an alliance with the northwestern warlord Feng Yuxiang (Feng Yu-hsiang), and they armed his forces. The strength of the Communists' Guomindang left allies revived, especially after the Nationalist government moved to Wuhan (Hankow) on the middle Chang Jiang (Yangtze) in later 1926. Yet although the Communists were attracting mass support, they really controlled only one regiment in the whole Nationalist army, and their position, in the event of a new showdown, was not really strong. Having a distorted view of Chinese events, Stalin failed to recognize this, partly because of failings by his agents, but also because of the blinkers imposed by Marxist-Leninist doctrine. He saw the conflict in China in terms of categories such as "feudalism" and the "bourgeoisie," where they did not apply. He apparently overrated the Chinese Communists' ability to subvert the Nationalist army, he overrated the power of the Guomindang left, and he continued to suppose that Jiang was far more dependent on the Soviet Union than he really was. On one occasion Stalin compared Jiang to a lemon, which could be squeezed dry and then thrown away. He forbade an attempt to form a separate Communist army, although most of the officers in the Nationalist army were landlords and were increasingly upset at Communist-organized peasant agitation. Yet for a time purely political maneuvers seemed to be going well. In March 1927 Wang and the Guomindang left deprived Jiang of his position as party chairman, replacing this post with a "presidium" led by Wang.

Jiang refused to submit to this. He was launching a maneuver of his own. In March 1927, under Communist leadership the labor movement of Shanghai rose against the forces of the local warlord and drove them out. Jiang held his forces nearby and let his enemies weaken each other. The warlord beaten, Jiang occupied Shanghai. The Communists received incoherent orders from Moscow. They were ordered neither to resist Jiang by force nor bury their weapons; instead, they were to bury them. On April 12 Jiang's forces, joining with secret societies and gangsters, simply massacred the labor forces. With Shanghai's factories and revenue under his control and having come to terms with the merchants and bankers of the coastal ports and the foreign powers, Jiang no longer needed Soviet help. There was now a formal break as Jiang set up a separate government at Nanking. It and the Guomindang left government at Wuhan, now including Communist ministers, both claimed to be the true government of China. Stalin was in the last stages of his fight with Trotsky, and the latter's often justified attacks on his policies in China merely made Stalin more obstinate. Instead of cutting his losses and allowing the Chinese Communists to regain their freedom of action, Stalin frantically insisted on maintaining the alliance with the Guomindang left. He hoped that the Communists could take the Wuhan government over from within, maintaining the Guomindang as a front and adding its forces to those of the Communists. Stalin "explained" his policy in class terms, claiming that Jiang's defection merely meant that the "big bourgeoisie" had defected from the revolution; the Guomindang left represented the "petty bourgeoisie" and would stay loyal. In fact there was little difference in composition between the two regimes, and the same forces that had impelled Jiang to break with the Communists were operating in the Wuhan government areas. It too depended on armed forces connected with landlords fearful of the Communists. On June 1 Stalin sent a rather incoherent message to M. N. Roy, the Comintern representative at Wuhan, ordering him to undertake decisive steps to control the Guomindang left regime. Whereas Stalin overrated the strength of the Wuhan regime and its value to the Communists, Roy believed it was so weak that it had no choice but to submit to the Soviet-Communist terms. He later maintained that Wang nearly did submit. Overconfident, Roy showed Stalin's message to Wang. But Wang was already in contact with Jiang Jieshi, and he decided to come to terms with him instead. The Guomindang left turned on and crushed the Communists, as did Feng Yuxiang. During the next few months the Communists tried to regroup, staging several futile uprisings, some perhaps ordered by Stalin just to provide propaganda stunts to assist him in his battle with the Soviet opposition. These merely led to the destruction of much of what was left of the Chinese Communist party. Some of the survivors went underground to try to rebuild the party's strength in the cities. Others fled to the countryside to start guerrilla warfare.[3]

In Indonesia, or as it then was, the Netherlands East Indies, a policy of alliance with the Sarekat Islam nationalist group, similar to the alliance with the Guomindang, helped the local Communists become a serious force. But after breaking with Sarekat Islam the Communists followed a muddled policy. In 1926 they wrecked themselves by launching an abortive uprising that was quickly crushed by the Dutch. The orthodox, pro-Moscow Communists did not recover as a serious force until after World War II. But an element of the Communist party, led by Tan Malaka, the Comintern agent for Southeast Asia, broke away. It rejected Moscow's authority and formed a "national communist" group more influential than the Stalinists.[4]

Unlike the Indonesian Communists, the Chinese quickly bounced back from disaster, but as peasant-based guerrillas rather than as an urban, worker-oriented movement. The most successful of its leaders was Mao Zedong, who had been closely associated with the peasant movement during the alliance with the Guomindang and who founded a guerrilla base in the mountains of Jiangsi (Kiangsi). However, for several years the principal leaders of the

Chinese Communist party remained in Shanghai. Although the Comintern thoroughly approved of guerrilla warfare as a holding action, it hoped that the party in the cities could be rebuilt as a major force. Mao Zedong himself conceived of his actions in these terms. He was not fixated on guerrilla warfare and from the first tried to build up a regular Red Army with heavy weapons. The party's leaders distrusted the peasants on doctrinal grounds; at first they tried to base their support in the countryside only on poor peasants and landless farm workers. Following a very radical land policy, they sought to seize and redistribute all land in the areas under their control. In the first of several violent fluctuations of land policy, they shifted in 1929 to confiscating only the property of the landlords; Mao went further and in areas under his control tried to base the party on the support of the richest strata of the peasantry. The guerrillas, operating in the interior of South-Central China, were only loosely controlled by the central Party organization and were often badly divided among themselves. On some occasions full-scale battles occurred between Communist factions.

The Comintern replaced the former leaders of the party—scaspegoats for the disasters of 1927—with Li Lisan, a man whose power base lay in what was left of the Communist city organizations. Li proceeded to ignore the directives of the Comintern, which had envisaged a prolonged period of guerrilla war before a final victory in China. Li insisted that a major revolutionary situation was developing and a quick victory was possible. He planned to launch a series of strikes, to be followed by an uprising in the cities supported by attacks by the Red Army. Evading attempts by the Comintern to stop him, Li launched his uprising in 1930. The Red Army managed to take the city of Changsha for a time but was soon thrown out. Li was finally sacked and exiled to Moscow. A group of Soviet-trained Chinese Communists, the "Russian Returned Student" faction, led by Chen Shaoyu (better known under the pseudonym "Wang Ming") began to take control of the party, which henceforth stuck to guerrilla warfare in comparatively remote areas. The Communists repelled several clumsy Nationalist attempts to attack their principal base in Jiangsi while feuding among themselves. Mao, originally the principal leader in Jiangsi, was eclipsed by those associated with the Russian Returned Students. When a "Chinese Soviet Republic" was proclaimed in November 1931, he played only a small role. By 1932 the Chinese Soviet forces numbered 150,000 armed men and posed a major threat to the Nationalists.[5]

The Nationalists, however, were ready to counter the threat. That the Communists were ultimately the victors in the struggle for China should not disguise the fact that the Nationalist-Communist competition was very much a competition in who would organize China, and in the first stages of this struggle, until the outbreak of full-scale war with Japan in 1937, the Nationalists were very much more successful. In 1928 Jiang Jieshi, at first paying little attention to the remnants of the apparently beaten Communists, had nominally unified China under the rule of the Guomindang. The subsequent "Nanking decade," so-called because the capital in that era was at Nanking instead of the traditional Beijing, saw considerable progress, although it is debatable how much of this could be credited to the policies of the Nationalist government. Considerable economic development took place in China's coastal cities. However, the Nationalists ignored the problems of rural areas, and this contributed greatly to their final defeat. They rejected the idea of land reform. Essentially they did nothing about the problems of the peasantry, although, as Lloyd Eastman has noted, modest reforms such as the rationalization of the land tax system "would have measurably improved the lives of the majority of the farmers (and) could have been accomplished by the Nationalist government without undertaking such radical structural changes as land redistribution."[6] The government tended to favor the interests of the landlords; thus, for example, laws designed to reduce rents were never enforced. The regime did not develop a popular base or even gain the support of any particular class. Some elements of the left wing of the Guomindang, notably Wang Jingwei's "Reorganization Faction," urged land reform and the transformation of the Guomindang into a democratic party with a mass base. But the Reorganization Faction was never very successful in intraparty factional struggles. It was ultimately discredited when Wang advocated appeasing Japan and finally defected to the Japanese during the Sino-Japanese War.[7]

Nevertheless, the Nationalist government was in a strong position. For some years Jiang was distracted from the Communist problem by uprisings of warlord forces and dissident Guomindang factions. But in 1933–34, he turned his strength against the Communists. Assisted by a very capable German military mission, the Nationalists concentrated strong forces in Jiangsi. They ringed the Communist area with blockhouses linked by barbed wire and other defensive positions and imposed a complete economic blockade. The blockade caused great hardships for the Red Army and the "Soviet" population, and the Nationalist armies slowly compressed the Communist territory; several *million* people may have died in the course of this campaign. It became apparent that Jiangsi must be evacuated.

In October 1934 a force of 100,000 soldiers and civilians left the Jiangsi base, leaving some stay-behind parties of guerrillas. At first the Communists had no clear idea of their ultimate destination. In January 1935 Mao Zedong took control over the party from the Russian Returned Students, who had been weakened by the recent military defeats. Under Mao's leadership, the larger portion of the Communist forces set out for a small Communist-controlled area in the barren Shaaxi-Gansu area of northern China. In October 1935, after an epic march of 6,000 miles and many battles with pursuing Nationalist forces, 20,000 people arrived in Shaaxi.[8] The Communists had reached their nadir, and the base from which they would ultimately rise to rule China.

Europe in the 1930s

From a later perspective the most prominent features of the early 1930s were the rise of nazism and the beginning of Japanese aggression against China. The Soviets seem to have paid very little attention to the Nazis and in general played an inactive role in international affairs. Stalin apparently now had little confidence in the ability of foreign Communists to accomplish much and reportedly referred contemptuously to the Comintern as the *lavochka* (the little shop). He concentrated his attention on the collectivization of agriculture and the Five Year Plan. The "extreme left" line introduced in 1928 was continued and even intensified. Communist parties fiercely attacked democratic socialists as the main enemy. While paying little attention to genuine fascist movements, they hysterically denounced socialists as "social-fascists," the worst fascists of all. The nadir of the Great Depression might have seemed to be a great opportunity for the Communists, but this did not prove to be the case. It was only in 1934 and the following years that Communism and the Soviet Union gained prestige and followers in most Western democratic countries. When economic conditions were at their worst, people (except in Germany) may have actually been too desperate to contemplate radical change, while the irrationality of Communist propaganda in the early 1930s did not encourage confidence in Communism as a solution. Perhaps only after the Depression had bottomed out did people have time to think; then disgust with the apparent collapse of capitalism took full effect, and the contrast between economic collapse in the West and the rapid industrialization of the Soviet Union, with its purportedly rationally planned economy, seemed telling. And during the Popular Front era, the Communists appeared more reasonable and appealing than they had earlier. In the early 1930s the strength of most Communist parties in the West actually declined; Germany proved the major and short-lived exception to this decline. In Germany a real revolutionary situation seemed to develop, and in fact a real revolutionary situation did develop— with the slight but crucial qualification that it was a fascist revolution, not a Communist one.

During the early 1930s the Comintern and the German Communists continued all-out attacks against the Social Democrats and the Weimar Republic as the main obstacles to a Communist seizure of power. The growing strength of the Nazi party was interpreted as a symptom of disintegration; the Communists insisted that even if the Nazis established their rule, they would not be able to handle the economic crisis and would soon fall, having acted as the "icebreaker of revolution" for the Communists, who were expected to survive any brief period of persecution easily. In practice, the Communist efforts converged with those of the Nazis. The two parties even cooperated actively, calling for a referendum to bring down the Prussian state government. The Communists joined with the Nazis in the Berlin transport strike of 1932. The Nazi and Communist private armies, the SA (Stürmabteilung) and the Rotefrontkampferbund, jointly attacked the meetings of democratic groups. The Communists' "illegal" organizations redoubled their efforts, which were not very effective, to subvert the police and the army and obtain arms and explosives for a new attempt to seize power. Important factions in the German Communist party opposed this policy, but the Comintern overrode their objections, and it was continued to the bitter end. On January 30, 1933, Hitler became chancellor of Germany. The Communists had miscalculated their ability to survive attack; too many of their members were well-known, and the "cells" composing the underground party organization were too large and easily infiltrated. Most of all, however, they had underestimated Nazi ruthlessness and determination. Within a few months the Communist party, like every other political group, had been completely crushed. The blundering attempt to launch a Communist revolution in Germany had backfired, contributing to the rise of a deadly threat to the Soviet Union.

It is possible, however, that the rise of Hitler was not unwelcome to Stalin and that this was the *intended* consequence of the policy forced on the German Communists. Some former leaders of the German Communist party later maintained that Stalin did not believe his followers could take power in Germany. They believed that he wished the Nazis to take over because they would rearm Germany and eventually produce a major war in the West, thus opening the way for Soviet expansion.[1]

For a while Stalin may have thought that the Nazi regime was only a passing phase or that it would merely be a front for reactionary forces and the German army, who would wish to maintain or even develop the special relationship between Germany and the Soviet Union. Such groups would favor a war of revenge against the Western powers and Poland. However, Hitler proved violently hostile to the Soviet Union. After Hitler's massacre of his enemies in and outside the Nazi party in June 1934, Stalin decided that the Nazi regime would last. He had begun taking limited steps to counter the danger of further fascist seizures of power and German and Japanese aggression.

Japan, unlike Germany, was well-armed and with the seizure of Manchuria in 1931–32 presented a far more immediate threat. Although like the Western powers the Soviet Union was unwilling to aid China seriously because of the risk of war with Japan, Stalin moved during 1932 to restore diplomatic relations with Jiang Jieshi. The Japanese threat was a major factor in the Roosevelt administration's decision to establish diplomatic relations with the Soviet Union. However, the resulting relationship proved disappointing to both sides. The United States had developed an able group of experts on Soviet affairs at its diplomatic mission at Riga in the 1920s, but these men were generally ignored, for their bleakly realistic views of the Soviet Union did not fit with the optimism fashionable in the West and especially inside the Roosevelt administration. President Roosevelt chose to send as his first ambassador William Bullitt, who had been enthusiastically pro-Soviet. Like many non-Communist foreigners forced into intimate contact with Stalin's regime, Bullitt was soon disillusioned and became bitterly anti-Soviet ever after. He was replaced by Joseph E. Davies, who was also pro-Soviet but lacked the intellectual caliber and honesty to change his mind. Despite the presence of able men such as George F. Kennan at the Moscow Embassy, the result of its establishment was the flow of pap rather than useful information to Washington.

At the end of 1933 the Comintern began to stop the campaign against "social fascism" and began concentrating attacks on the genuine article. The Soviet Union moved to join the League of Nations and establish loose alliances with the Western powers. During 1935 the Soviets negotiated alliances with France and Czechoslovakia. But the alliance with France, which was the crucial arrangement, was never ratified by the upper house of the French parliament. The Soviet foreign minister, Maxim Litvinov, became an outspoken advocate of "collective security" against aggression, although the Soviets were extremely cautious about committing themselves to clear-cut military action. However, Litvinov's eloquent speeches made a favorable impression on public opinion in the democracies, for many were increasingly disgusted with the feebleness and confusion of the Western governments.[2]

In February 1934 the somewhat exaggerated threat of a fascist takeover in France caused the Comintern to experiment with a new version of the united front in that country. (During 1933 the Chinese Communists in Manchuria, but not in the rest of China, had been allowed to form united fronts with non-Communist groups in order to resist the Japanese.) The French Communist party was permitted to approach as allies in a "Popular Front" not only socialists but also liberals—something never tried before in advanced countries. The new line proved remarkably successful. When the Communists won considerable victories at local elections in France in May 1935, they became for the first time a party with mass support. Their growth was largely at the expense of their Socialist and Radical allies. This unexpected triumph revived some of Stalin's faith in the value of foreign Communist parties. In July-August 1935 the Comintern's Seventh (and last) Congress extended the Popular Front antifascist line to the entire world. Communists were instructed to draw a clear distinction between "bourgeois democracy" and fascist dictatorship. A major shift in terminology took place, and Communists began substituting in their public statements a liberal-sounding, pseudo-democratic vocabulary for Leninist terms. The Seventh Congress marked a permanent change in tactics for the world's Communist parties; for although the Popular Front itself soon expired, they permanently abandoned the idea of organizational isolation imposed in the 1920s. Communists could now form any political alliance that seemed tactically suitable and could now accept positions in coalition governments.

The Soviet Union and the Comintern appeared to be committed to a fundamentally defensive policy strongly opposed to fascism, a view of Soviet policy generally accepted both at the time and later. In fact, this view was a grave oversimplification on two levels. The new policy was not lacking in offensive possibilities. Speakers at the Seventh Comintern Congress discussed the possibility of using the antifascist struggle as a path to Communist seizures of power. Any war against a fascist power was to be used to spread the influence of the local Communist party and secure its participation in the government. Anticommunists should be purged from the state bureaucracy, army, and police. A Popular Front government was seen as a route to the creation of a "democracy of a new type." This term foreshadowed the designation "people's democracy," which was applied to the satellite states set up in Eastern Europe and Korea in the 1940s. At the Seventh Congress Dimitri Manuilsky, the behind-the-scenes chief of the Comintern, gave a classic expression of the traditional Communist approach to alliances and taking power, a stinging comment on those who saw the Popular Front line as a fundamental change to moderation: "There are those who imagine that in one place an army will line up and say, 'We are for socialism' and in another place another army will say 'We are for imperialism' and that this will be the social revolution. Whoever expects a 'pure' social revolution will *never* live to see it, such a person pays lip service to revolution without understanding what revolution means."[3]

The widespread acceptance of the notion that the Soviets and their followers were committed to a firm policy of opposition to fascism and had even dropped the idea of world revolution altogether in favor of the defense of democracy and reformism was mistaken in yet another way. Stalin himself never liked the antifascist line or the Popular Front. Indeed, the history of the Communist party prepared under his supervision and published in 1939 did not mention either the Seventh Comintern Congress or the Popular Front policy. Stalin seems always to have disliked policies that brought Communists into close contact with socialists and liberals as endangering discipline and doctrinal sharpness. (Actually, united fronts and Popular Fronts seem to have consistently worked in favor of the Communists, not their "allies.") Stalin's personal preference was for policies of "left extremism" or, better yet, alliances with the extreme right. His fascination with the latter idea was the true key to his policy in the 1930s.

The antifascist line was a *pis aller* that he reluctantly adopted as a means to attain his real aim, or at most as an insurance policy should that aim prove unattainable. His real goal was to come to an arrangement with Hitler. The policy of bolstering resistance to Nazism was primarily a way to force Hitler to negotiate. Stalin secretly tried several times from 1935 to 1937, mostly under cover of trade missions, to encourage Hitler to come to terms. It was Hitler's hatred of the Soviets, not Soviet hostility to fascism, that delayed a Nazi-Soviet agreement until 1939. These facts were disclosed as early as 1938 by Walter Krivitsky, the Soviet intelligence chief in the Netherlands, and confirmed later by German documents.[4] The fantastic Great Purges begun by Stalin in 1936 were aimed originally at destroying any Soviet leaders and elements of the high command who might oppose a deal with Hitler. Stalin ironically accused his victims of plotting with the Nazis—the very policy he favored himself. Interestingly, however, the 1938 Trial of the "Bukharin-Right-Trotskyite bloc" accused those on trial of conspiring not only with Germany and Japan but with Britain; they allegedly plotted to hand Central Asia over to the British. Despite this and much other evidence that the charges were false, the belief that Stalin's victims were guilty was dumbly accepted by many in the West.

The purge of the armed forces would indeed have been inconceivable had Stalin expected a major war to break out in a few years or even seriously worried about this possibility. Three of the five marshals of the Soviet Union, all eight Soviet admirals, 14 of 16 army commanders, 60 of 67 corps commanders, 136 of 199 division commanders, 221 of 397 brigade commanders—in all, half the Soviet officer corps—became victims of the Great Purges. In addition, a large proportion of the foreign Communists residing in the Soviet Union, especially refugees from the Axis powers and their allies, were killed or imprisoned. The Comintern's headquarters were practically wiped out. The Polish Communist party was particularly hard hit and was actually dissolved—possibly part of the preparations for a Nazi-Soviet partition of that country.

However, it may be a mistake to attach too much rational purpose to the Great Purges, for they soon degenerated into a blind convulsion of destruction. Stalin wiped out not merely his beaten rivals but his own original supporters and reformed the Communist party out of the terrorized remnants. Less than 2 percent of the delegates to the Seventeenth Party Congress in 1934 reappeared at the next Congress in 1939. The ruling organ of the Soviet state was transformed in his image and into his personal tool.

The Great Purges were accompanied by a vast expansion of the Soviet concentration camp system into a major factor in the Soviet economy. After 1937 there were probably never less than 7 million prisoners, with a quarter of a million guards, in slave labor camps. After World War II, when the system became a major tool in the subjugation of Eastern Europe, the number of prisoners rose to a probable maximum total of 12 to 14 million in the early 1950s. Even before World War II, according to the state economic plan for 1941—an incomplete copy of which was captured by the Nazis—slave labor encompassed 18 percent or more of the Soviet economy.[5] The Great Purges, the rise of the slave labor empire, and the collectivization and industrialization drives marked the crystallization of Stalin's second revolution and the system he intended to export to the rest of the world. Late in his life he did contemplate launching new internal upheavals—a new Great Purge, the deportation of the Jews, and the consolidation of the collective farms as *agrogorodnys*—but the priority attached to foreign affairs and his death prevented a new series of horrors.

The lengths to which Stalin let the Great Purges go were hardly the acts of a rational man, and his pursuit of a deal with Hitler might well seem crazy in view of Hitler's obvious anticommunism and intention, well-publicized in *Mein Kampf,* of conquering the Soviet Union. However, we now look back at the 1930s "past" the dramatic Nazi victories of 1940 and 1941, events which were expected by very few people before they happened. Stalin was not uniquely wrong headed. Like almost everyone else, he underestimated Nazi strength until May 1940. The quick defeat of France came as a great shock to the Soviets, as the Soviet ambassador in Stockholm openly admitted in June 1940. At the Eighteenth Party Congress in March 1939 Stalin stressed that the Western democracies were much stronger than the aggressors.[6] Nazi Germany was seen as a danger of sorts, but not a singularly overwhelming one. It was best coped with by directing it against the Western powers, where its aggressive tendencies would actually serve Soviet interests. The Western powers would tie down the Germans; the Maginot line, the probable rough equality of forces on the Western front, and the experiences of World War I in the West, all suggested that a clear German victory was unlikely.

The political geography of Eastern Europe between the world wars seemed to favor Stalin's policy. Unlike Britain and France, the Soviets were separated from Germany by a broad belt of Polish and Romanian territory. Both those countries were allied to France; and unless the French completely abandoned their allies, Germany could not conquer them without triggering a war with the West. In practice, a major German invasion of the Soviet Union could only come through Poland. As a prelude to a Russian campaign Hitler had to make Poland a reliable satellite or conquer her. At first Hitler seemed to want an alliance with the Poles; whereas after their initial proposals for a preventive war against Germany were rejected by the French, the Polish leaders seemed to be seeking a position of neutrality or even a limited collaboration with Germany. Even this policy was violently unpopular in Poland, and no Polish leaders were willing simply to submit to Germany. All Poles knew that a real alliance with Germany would be an attempt to ride a very big and hungry tiger, and Polish policy between the world wars was to allow neither German nor Soviet troops in their country, a policy the Soviets understood by 1936 if not earlier.[7] If Germany attacked Poland and France adhered to her alliance, the Germans would be neatly tied down without any need for Soviet action. Conversely, it would have been difficult for Stalin to act effectively against Germany even had he wanted to. The Soviets could help neither the Czechs nor the Western European powers because the Poles and Romanians refused to allow the passage of Soviet forces. In any event Stalin had little stomach for engaging in a *defensive* war, especially one that might turn into a two-front war. He was deeply conscious that the Japanese were an immediate threat to the Soviet Far East, where there was no buffer of territory between the U.S.S.R. and the aggressor. Nor did Stalin feel too secure in the saddle; since a German or Japanese entry into Soviet territory might well encourage rebellion by nationalist or anticommunist elements. Stalin could not know in the 1930s that the Nazis' own ideological insanities would prevent them from playing such cards in a serious way.

There was, of course, some danger that the Western powers might abandon Eastern Europe out of cowardice, short-sightedness, or the hope that the Nazis would become involved in a war with the Soviets. Yet such a policy might result in the Nazis turning against the West, instead; and if the Germans destroyed the Soviet Union, the West would face an even worse long-term threat. The Western powers could in no way profit from German expansion. Unlike Stalin, they could not gain anything by partitioning territory with Germany. Soviet policies of the Popular Front era were an effort to push the West into doing what it was likely to do anyway in self-defense. Once the West decided to resist Nazi expansion, Hitler would be forced to deal with Stalin and offer a partition of Eastern Europe. The Western powers' appeasement policies may well have given Stalin some bad moments, but basic geopolitical factors favored a Nazi-Soviet pact. It was not an "historical accident" but the natural product of the European situation and Hitler's and Stalin's aims.

A pact with Germany and a war in the West would neutralize the Nazi threat and provide Stalin with what he had long looked forward to: an exhausting war that would create opportunities for expansion and revolutionary situations, allowing him to establish Soviet domination over most or even all of Europe. Until the unexpected defeat of France in 1940, his hopes seemed well on the way to realization.

An alternative explanation of Soviet policy, popular in the 1930s and 1940s and sometimes heard even today, is that Stalin was genuinely opposed to Nazi Germany and was forced to deal with Hitler in 1939 only by the West's policies of appeasement, especially by the sellout of Czechoslovakia at Munich. However, not only is this argument contradicted by the German records showing earlier approaches, it is incompatible with the actual sequence of events. The arrangement with Germany was made, not right after Munich, but months after the appeasement policy had been abandoned and the British had guaranteed to fight if Germany attacked Poland and Romania and, in effect, the Soviet Union. Nor did Stalin behave in 1939–40 like a man who had dealt with Germany reluctantly only to deflect a desperate danger. Rather, he viewed a quasi-alliance with Germany as a basic policy. He acted as though the Germans were the weaker side in the war, a view of the situation he had endorsed publicly, and he leaned toward the Nazis to counter the apparently greater weight of resources enjoyed by the democracies.

The Japanese invasion of Manchuria and Hitler's rise to power reduced the Soviet Union to a relatively minor problem as far as the Western European democracies were concerned. Their policy of appeasement was not directed toward "pushing Germany eastward," as is sometimes still claimed. Some persons in Britain and France did think along such lines, but they did not make policy. Appeasement was based on an unrealistic view of Nazi Germany, not on hostility to communism. Many on the French right did work themselves into near hysteria about communism, especially after the formation of a Popular Front government in France in 1936, although they generally failed to distinguish between the Communists and the Socialists, who were actually the dominant force in the government. Yet distaste for communism and an alliance with the Soviet government was merely another argument for appeasement policies founded on other beliefs. There was no fear of Soviet aggression. The British government was not much worried about Communist subversion by the 1930s, and it had a low opinion of the strength of the Soviet state. Robert Vansittart, the permanent undersecretary of the Foreign Office, expressed a general view when he wrote in 1934 that "Russia has been too incompetent a country to be really dangerous, even under Bolshevism. But Germany is an exceedingly competent country." Sir Neville Chamberlain, the prime minister of Britain from 1937–40, and some others did fear the Soviets would seek to contrive a situation in which the Nazis and the Western European democracies would exhaust themselves in war. Chamberlain viewed this as yet another argument for appeasement.[8] But Germany, and to a lesser extent Japan and Italy, formed the focus of attention for the Western democracies. Fear of fascist aggression, or the desperate and futile hope of avoiding war, not the threat of the Soviet Union or communism, dominated the thoughts of the Western world.

The Popular Front did not influence public opinion in favor of the Soviet Union and communism, and it resulted in concrete political alliances in only a few countries. France, Spain, China, and the resistance movement to the clerical rightist dictatorship in Austria saw the only effective Popular Front coalitions. In general, most socialists and liberals in other countries welcomed the Communist stand against fascism but were too wary of the Communists to form close ties with them. Nor were the Popular Fronts smoothly functioning alliances. Behind the scenes the French Popular Front government was torn by bitter hostility and intrigue. Neither the Communists nor the democratic left actually followed through with effective action against the Axis powers. The democratic left in France and other Western countries often treated fascism as primarily an *internal* threat. They often focused their attention, not on the real danger of German and Italian aggression, but on the vastly exaggerated threat of seizures of power by local fascist parties. Their obsession was with subversion rather than external events. (There is an interesting parallel here with McCarthyism in the early 1950s.) Moreover, pacifism and hostility to the military made them oppose rearmament and other serious measures to cope with the real external threat. The Communists in France were at best ambiguous in their attitude to defense. They opposed lengthening the term of service for draftees and the introduction of longer hours in war industries. These and other peculiarities of Communist policy in France and Spain seem to be related to Stalin's aim of striking a deal with Germany.[9]

The Popular Front government formed in Spain in 1936 bore only a superficial resemblance to that in France. Ironically, a truly revolutionary situation in a European country, for which the Comintern had sought in vain for so long, arrived in a form and at a time when it was undesirable. Spain was a relatively backward land with a major agrarian problem and riven by regional conflicts. The Popular Front government was nominally run by middle-class Republicans, but the incompetent Republican leaders had alienated even moderate conservatives by their refusal or inability to control terrorism by left-wing fanatics. The government really rested on a very narrow basis of support, for the Spanish Socialist party had become extremely radicalized and was hostile to the middle-class left. Adopting Leninism, it differed from an orthodox

Communist party principally in its refusal to follow Moscow's orders blindly and in its lack of discipline. Unlike any other Western country, Spain had a powerful anarchosyndicalist movement. The Spanish Communist party was small but rapidly gaining in strength thanks to its superior discipline. All these groups, including the Communists, believed that Spain was in the grip of a revolutionary situation comparable to that of Russia in 1917 and that things were becoming ripe for their seizure of power.

A rapid and ugly polarization between right and left ended in a reactionary military revolt on July 17, 1936. The "Nationalist" coup was only partly successful. In part of Spain the Republican government held on, often in name only. For the revolt of the right had sparked an effective seizure of power by the extreme left. The Axis powers, seeing a chance to make mischief, promptly intervened. Hitler had no burning interest in Spain, but he realized that a prolonged war there would serve as a useful tool. It would divide public opinion in the democracies, divert attention from more important German moves in Central Europe, and serve as a testing ground for German tactics and weapons. He left the main burden of supporting the Nationalists to Mussolini.[10]

The Soviets may have sent a small shipment of weapons to Spain as early as late July 1936, but Stalin was reluctant to involve the Soviet Union in Spain on a major scale. He hoped the French would support the Republicans, deepening the conflict between the Axis powers and the democracies. The French sent only token aid, and the Western powers reacted to the war by launching a farcical "nonintervention" agreement, which the Axis powers promptly violated.

This presented Stalin with a difficult problem. Either too strong an intervention in Spain or doing nothing could damage the Soviet Union's international position. Late in August he decided to intervene in Spain on a limited scale. The probable reasoning behind the decision was the need to support the Popular Front strategy, maintain Soviet prestige, and perhaps secure some sort of bargaining point that might be useful in a deal with the Nazis. Stalin may also have objected to the sight of a left-wing revolutionary movement taking place outside the Soviet-controlled Comintern framework; a Soviet intervention in Spain would help the Spanish Communists gain control of and curb this movement. Yet too great an involvement and too open a support for the Spanish Communists would help appeasers in the West, so Soviet aid had to be limited. Thus a decisive effort to transform Spain into a permanent, openly Communist satellite was not possible. Already in July the Spanish Communists had reverted to a more moderate line, advocating the "defense of the Republic" against the Nationalists and rejecting any social revolutionary measures. The Communists emerged as a party on the *extreme right* of the Republican coalition—a most unusual position for Communists. (However, this odd situation was later partially duplicated in Chile under Allende.) They allied themselves with what was left of the Republicans proper and attracted a membership of middle-class people, officials, and soldiers.

The Comintern embarked on the task of disguising the violent and conflict-ridden regime in the Republican zone as a reformist "bourgeois-democratic" government defending itself against the attacks of German and Italian puppets. Ignorant liberals and left-wingers in the Western world readily swallowed this version of events or let wishful thinking guide them along parallel lines. In general, public opinion attached a wildly exaggerated importance to the Spanish Civil War.[11] As Arthur Koestler observed in his autobiography, "Compared to Germany, Spain was a small and peripheral country, and yet Franco unleashed a wave of more passionate indignation throughout the world than Hitler during the initial stages of his regime." The British diplomat Fitzroy Maclean was amazed to find that the French public apparently attached more importance to Spain than to the Nazi reoccupation of the Rhineland![12] Given this state of mind, Stalin's limited and realpolitik-oriented moves in Spain were a tremendous propaganda success, convincing many that the Soviet Union was a more reliable bulwark against the spread of fascism than the democracies. The government of the latter seemed impotent, even laughable, in their devotion to the fatuous nonintervention agreements.

The first Soviet moves in Spain undoubtedly prevented the early defeat of the Republican forces. Once the decision to intervene was made, the Soviets rushed weapons to Spain; their tanks and planes proved to be of higher quality than those yet available to the Nazis. Soviet secret police agents and a Soviet military mission arrived. The latter numbered no more than 700 men at any one time and consisted mostly of staff officers, technicians, and pilots using elaborate disguises to hide their identities. As they did later in the Sino-Japanese War and the Korean War, the Soviets used the air fighting as a training ground, rapidly rotating pilots as soon as they gained combat experience. The Soviet mission gained effective control of the Republican air force and tank corps, as well as a large measure of influence over the Spanish operations in general. Along with the Spanish Communists they forced the left-wing extremists to accept a restoration of some discipline and rational organization among the Republican forces. The Comintern organized the famous "International Brigades" for service in Spain. Initially built around a cadre of German Communist refugees drafted in the Soviet Union, the brigades received 35,000 volunteers from many different countries, mostly Communists or Communist sympathizers. The International Brigades provided a principal instrument of Soviet power, a "proxy force" comparable to that later provided by satellite states such as Cuba during the cold war. Soviet arms and the arrival of the International Brigades saved Madrid from capture by the Nationalists. The Soviets' near-monopoly of aid to the Republicans gave them a stranglehold over the government.

With their support the Spanish Communists were able to crush the far left and gain effective control over the government by mid-1937. Their political tactics bore some resemblances to those later used in the first stages of the seizure of power in post–World War II Eastern Europe. Once a collapse had been averted and Soviet domination established, however, Stalin clearly lost interest in Spain. He let the Republicans gradually succumb to the Nationalists and their Axis allies. Soviet aid to the Republicans was reduced, and the Soviet effort in Spain was violently disrupted by the Great Purges. Most officials and officers who had served there were killed, and the Red Army misinterpreted the lessons of the war. The war did help to build up Communist power in the West. It gave the cadres of some Communist parties military experience that proved valuable in the resistance movements during World War II and tied them more tightly into the Soviet intelligence network. On the whole, however, the war was a bloody fiasco for the Soviets, save in its propaganda aspects.[13]

After the cutback in their effort in Spain, the Soviets did not play a very active role in European affairs. Meanwhile, the Nazis and the Western democracies moved toward war. The latter continued, as Churchill once put it, to "present a front of two overripe melons crushed together." In November 1937 Hitler conferred with senior military leaders and officials and announced an important decision. He had decided that the final drive for *Lebensraum* in the east would be launched by 1943–45. But well before that Germany must absorb Austria and Czechoslovakia. He had decided that although the British and French would let him grab those countries without fighting, they would oppose any further expansion eastward. The threat posed by the Western powers would have to be dealt with *before* the final drive to the east. Thus the Western powers, not the Soviets, would be the primary target once central Europe was taken.[14]

Hitler took Austria without any trouble. The move against Czechoslovakia proved more difficult, leading to a major international crisis. During that crisis the Western powers showed no sign of seeking to invoke Soviet help, and the Soviets remained rather passive. They were allied to Czechoslovakia, but their guarantee to that country had to be honored only if France came to the aid of the Czechs. The Soviets several times stated their readiness to carry out their obligations, though they never made clear just how they would do this. This was not surprising, since Poland and Romania flatly refused to let Soviet ground forces pass through their countries. Not in a position to stop them, the Romanians were willing to allow Soviet planes to fly over their territory and possibly let through supplies. The Soviets did warn the Poles, whose leaders planned to grab the Teschen area from Czechoslovakia, not to attack the Czechs. The Soviets were technically faithful to their alliances and were often later credited with being willing to fight in Czechoslovakia's defense. Yet their stance was not compatible with a serious readiness for war. The Soviet press made no attempt to prepare the population for war. *Pravda* actually criticized the Czech government for ordering a mobilization, while the French Communists attacked the French government on August 31 for trying to introduce longer hours in war industries.[15]

The Soviets violently denounced the Munich agreement, which ceded the German-populated border areas of Czechoslovakia to Germany, leaving the rest of the country at the mercy of the Nazis. It was clear that nothing could prevent Hitler from securing the rest of Czechoslovakia, whether by annexing it or turning it into a puppet state, and that Poland would almost certainly be the next target in Eastern Europe. A German subjugation of Poland would expose the Soviet Union to direct attack. Stalin may well have feared that the Western powers would give Hitler a free hand in the east. Actually, Hitler still planned to turn on the Western powers once Poland was either conquered or reduced to satellite status. The Soviets soon learned of this through their intelligence.[16]

In March 1939 Stalin made a public gesture to Germany at the Eighteenth Party Congress. (No one was left alive who was likely to object.) He accused the Western powers, including the United States, albeit in an ambiguous way, of trying to push Germany against the Soviet Union. While stressing that the "nonaggressive democratic states" were stronger than the aggressor countries, he also strongly implied there existed no real difference between this group of states and the Axis; his expressions of hostility toward the appeasers and their alleged motives were far harsher than his attacks on the Nazis. Stalin declared that there was no real danger of a Nazi move against the Soviet Union and said that Soviet policy was "to be cautious and not to be drawn into conflicts by warmongers who are accustomed to have others pull the chestnuts out of the fires for them." But the Nazis did not react to this hint. Shortly afterward, the Soviets proposed to Britain and France that they discuss a triple alliance designed to guarantee Eastern Europe. The Western powers showed no interest.[17]

The German seizure of Bohemia and Moravia in mid-March 1939 was the finishing blow for appeasement. On March 31 the British reversed their traditional policy of avoiding commitments in Eastern Europe and unilaterally extended military guarantees to Poland and Romania. Soon they increased their military preparations, imposing an unprecedented peacetime draft. Relations between the democracies and the Nazis became visibly worse. Hitler increased his pressure on Poland and denounced the Anglo-German Naval Agreement, which had been one of the appeasers' purported successes.

British public opinion, which was remarkably optimistic about Soviet intentions, forced a mulishly reluctant British government to belatedly try to form an alliance with the Soviets. But the British had already wrecked whatever slight bargaining position the Western powers had had by guaranteeing Poland and Romania, and in effect the Soviets, before reaching an agreement with the Soviet Union. Between intelligence of the Nazis' actual intention and Chamberlain's guarantees, Stalin could be reasonably sure that Hitler would be tied down before he could get at the Soviet Union. His openness to talks with the West was merely added insurance and a measure to improve his bargaining position with the Nazis. The latter, however, were reluctant to come to terms. To ease the way, on May 3 Stalin replaced his foreign minister, Litvinov, a man of Jewish origin closely associated with the "antifascist" policies, with Vyacheslav Molotov, a man much closer to the dictator.

The failure of the negotiations between the Soviets and the Western powers has often been blamed on the latter. The Western powers certainly bungled their end of the negotiations; yet even master diplomats could not have achieved much in the circumstances. The British sent relatively low ranking officials to Moscow and responded sluggishly to Soviet proposals, but they found that the Soviets increased their demands every time the Western powers made a concession. The Soviets refused a simple triple alliance; talks for a political alliance finally deadlocked in July when the Western powers refused the terms of a guarantee to the Eastern European countries against "indirect aggression," terms that would have let the Soviets seize the area on a slim pretext. Negotiations about military arrangements deadlocked over Soviet demands that their troops be allowed to pass through Poland and Romania, which those countries refused to permit, as the Soviets had known they would all along. The Soviets also insisted that the British and French fleets enter the Baltic, an impossibility. The Western-Soviet talks were then overtaken by a far more successful set of negotiations.[18]

Hitler finally conceded the necessity of making a deal with the Soviets. Under cover of trade negotiations, Soviet-German talks began. The Soviets' main aim was now to be certain that full-scale war would break out between Germany and the West. On August 23 the Germans and the Soviets signed a "Nonaggression Pact." Its actual purpose belied its title. A secret protocol divided Eastern Europe between Germany and the Soviet Union. The Soviets were to have a free hand in Finland, Estonia, Latvia, eastern Poland, and "Bessarabia and southeastern Europe." The Nazis appear to have signed the protocol so hastily that they did not carefully consider, or even clarify, the meaning of this last clause. (After the fall of Poland the boundary was readjusted. The Germans swapped Lithuania for part of Poland.) The Nazis hoped that the news of the pact with the Soviets would persuade the British and French to leave Poland in the lurch. But the democracies were fed up with both Nazi conquests and promises; reluctantly, they decided to fight. Once this was clear, the cautious Soviets finally broke off the negotiations with the British and French. The Soviets also concluded a trade agreement with the Germans, very favorable to the latter, which enabled the Nazis to evade the consequences of the British blockade.[19] On September 1 the Germans invaded Poland; World War II began.

East Asia: The 1930s and After

Soviet relations with the Japanese were far less tinged with ambiguity than their dealings with the Nazis. Relations remained basically hostile. During the early 1930s as the Japanese settled down in Manchuria, the Soviets energetically built up their military forces in the Soviet Far East and improved the tenuous connection between the Far East and Europe while avoiding any overt action that might give the Japanese occasion for attack. In 1935 they sold the Chinese Eastern Railway in northern Manchuria to Japan. The Japanese were in any case turning their attention toward China, not the Soviet Union. The military groups associated with the seizure of Manchuria envisaged an eventual war with the Soviet Union, but their influence declined. Similar military activists in the Japanese forces long stationed in China aimed at carving off chunks of North China, whereas policy makers in Tokyo were more attracted to expansion in China and the south. The latter sought to turn China as a whole into a Japanese satellite state. In August 1936 the cabinet adopted a set of "Fundamental Principles of National Policy" emphasizing China and envisaging a "gradual advance" toward the "South Seas," a program that had the same relation to World War II in the East as Hitler's decisions of November 1937 did to the pattern of the war in the West.[1]

The Chinese Communists provided the Soviets with a small but useful tool against the Japanese, who were unintentionally to give the Communists the opportunity to seize power in China. Already in 1932 the Chinese Communists in Jiangsi had "declared war" on Japan. This was largely a propaganda stunt, for the nearest Japanese were a thousand miles away. But the Chinese Communist organization in Manchuria, which had only a loose connection with the national party, began to play a major role in the resistance to the Japanese there. Before the Japanese invasion the Communists had had little success in Manchuria, whose society and economy differed greatly from that of the rest of China. Manchuria was more industrialized and prosperous; although there were many poor farmers, there existed considerable social mobility. The first upsurge of guerrilla fighting against the Japanese arose under traditional local leaders, but their forces were soon crushed by the Japanese. In 1933 Moscow permitted the Manchurian Communists, unlike the rest of the Chinese Communist party, to adopt a broad united front policy based on anti-Japanese sentiment. With the old framework of society shattered by the Japanese, the Communists were successful at gaining domination over what was left of the resistance by 1935–36 and subsequently building up their own guerrilla forces. They may have received aid on a small scale from the Soviets. When the Sino-Japanese War broke out in 1937, patriotic outrage in Manchuria revived. The Communist guerrillas rose to a force of 30,000 or more. These develoments foreshadowed what was to occur in the rest of China, although the Chinese Communist effort in Manchuria had a different ending. The Japanese launched a brutal but skillfully planned antiguerrilla campaign. Mustering strong forces and making use of Manchuria's relatively good communications and their familiarity with this part of China, they forced much of the peasantry into "collective hamlets" under tight control. They cut off the guerrillas from the population. By early 1941 the guerrillas had been destroyed or forced to flee into the Soviet Far East.[2]

The main body of the Chinese Communist movement had arrived in Shaanxi not long after the Soviets had decreed the new

Popular Front policy. They offered to form an anti-Japanese united front with other groups, though at first reluctant to extend this to include their archenemy, Jiang Jieshi. In the Shaanxi area they rebuilt their armed strength to perhaps 40,000 men and invaded the neighboring province of Shanxi (Shansi) in February 1936. Jiang assembled a force of 150,000 men to assault the Shaanxi base area. He intended to repeat the methods that had proven successful in Jiangsi and finally crush the Communists or force them to flee to Outer Mongolia. He seemed to be on the verge of completing his tenaciously pursued but very unpopular policy of "internal pacification before resistance to external aggression."

But he made a fatal error. He wished to conserve his central army forces, the core of well-armed, German-trained units that were under his direct control, unlike most of the Chinese army. So he assigned the task of defeating the Communists to Zhang Xueliang (Chang Hsueh-liang), the exiled warlord of Manchuria, and a local warlord. Neither Zhang nor his men felt strongly against the Communists, however. Their desire was to fight the Japanese, and they were strongly attracted by the Communists' propaganda in favor of an anti-Japanese united front. They refused to launch an offensive; and in December 1936, when Jiang Jieshi went to Xi'an (Sian) to get the war against the Communists going, he was kidnapped by Zhang. The Communists, who had not been in on the plot, at first argued that Jiang should be tried and executed. But they were brought up short by Moscow, which wanted Jiang spared. The Soviets had no love for Jiang but apparently estimated that if he were eliminated, his probable successors were likely to come to terms with Japan. The Communists reluctantly reversed themselves. A bargain was struck, although it was never admitted by Jiang. He agreed to halt the anti-Communist war and resist further Japanese encroachments.

After intensive negotiations that lasted until September 1937 (well after the outbreak of the Sino-Japanese War), a formal agreement was reached between the Communists and the Nationalist government. A Communist representative joined the Nationalist "People's Political Council." The Communists agreed to submit nominally to government control, to dissolve the "Soviet Republic," and to accept that their forces would no longer constitute a separate Red Army but would be part of the Nationalist forces. Their forces were redesignated the "Eighth Route Army" and the name "Soviet" was no longer used to designate Communist base areas; the "Shaanxi-Gansu Soviet" was renamed the "Shaanxi-Gansu-Nlngxia Border Region." The Communists changed to a more moderate land policy in their areas, easing up on rich peasants and even landlords. Jiang Jieshi agreed to subsidize a Communist force of three divisions or 45,000 men (the Communists by this time actually had 80,000-90,000 troops) and even gave them some weapons.[3]

In August 1937, as the united front was being formed, the Soviets and Chiang's government signed a treaty that constituted a nonbelligerent alliance against Japan. The Soviets began a large-scale effort to aid the Nationalists, and, indeed, until 1941 the Soviet Union was China's chief source of external aid. The Soviets granted some $250 million in loans to the Nationalist government and supplied the Chinese with equipment for about ten infantry divisions and with at least 400 combat planes. Also, 500 Soviet military advisors were attached to the Nationalist army, serving in higher field headquarters and helping with tank, artillery, and flight training. The Soviets went further, sending four fighter and two bomber squadrons actually to fight the Japanese in 1937–38. Stalin almost completely refrained from supplying any direct aid to the Chinese Communist forces. Their location made such aid very difficult and in any case would have driven the Nationalists into the arms of the Japanese, with whom Jiang was negotiating in late 1937 and after. Soviet diplomats did intimate to Jiang that Soviet aid was dependent on avoiding civil war in China, and Stalin did exploit the Sino-Japanese War for expansionist purposes. Since 1933 the Soviets' influence in the Chinese Central Asian province of Xinjiang (Sinkiang) had grown. They had then helped its governor put down a native revolt. (Ninety-five percent of the area's population was non-Chinese.) During the Sino-Japanese War Soviet troops moved into Xinjiang, and Sheng was transformed into a puppet. Chinese Communists, including Mao Ze-dong's brother Zemin (Tse-min), were given important administrative posts. Soviet control over Xinjiang lasted until the Soviets were forced to evacuate the area during World War II.

The Soviets wished to avoid full-scale participation in the war. Yet in 1938 and 1939 there were two full-scale battles on the frontiers between the Soviet Union and Outer Mongolia and Manchuria. It has been widely held that these incidents were deliberately initiated by radical elements in the Japanese Kwantung Army in order to force the Tokyo government into war with the Soviets. However, the Kwantung Army leaders seem to have realized that Japan was not ready for such a war, and it is more likely that the incidents were deliberately blown up by both sides in an effort to "teach the other a lesson." The Soviets dealt summarily with both incidents, for their forces in the Far East were now considerably stronger than those of the Japanese in Manchuria. The second "frontier incident" at Khalkin Ghol (or Nomonhan) on the Mongolian border in May-September 1939 approached the dimensions of a major campaign. In a well-planned offensive in August 1939 that forced the Japanese to come to terms, the Soviet forces, ably directed by the future marshal Georgi Zhukov, employed more than 500 tanks. The Soviets won control of the air and inflicted a humiliating defeat on the Japanese, who suffered very heavy losses. This little-known battle may have had considerable influence on the course of World War II. In 1941 the Japanese leaders, unlike the rest of the world, showed little inclination to underestimate Soviet strength. They chose to move south rather than north at a time when an attack on the Soviet Union might well have finished off that country.[4]

During the mid-1930s and the first years of the Sino-Japanese War the Chinese Communists developed the main elements of what later became known as "Maoism," or, as the Chinese refer to it, the "thought of Mao Zedong"; these became the doctrinal foundation for their victory. Yet Mao's personal role and his originality have often been exaggerated. The Chinese Communists and their foreign admirers often credited him with ideological innovations and policies actually formulated earlier by Stalin; indeed, some of the concepts original to China were actually devised by the Communist generals Zhu De (Chu Teh) and Peng Dehuai (Peng Teh-huai) and the ideologist Chen Boda (Chen Po-ta). Mao did not prove grateful; Peng and Chen lived long enough to meet the same fate as Stalin's original supporters.

The most important element of Maoism was the elaboration of the theory of peasant-based revolutionary guerrilla warfare. The idea of a peasant base for revolution had already been accepted by Lenin, while the Comintern had endorsed guerrilla warfare as the road to victory in China as early as 1930. But a series of works produced from 1936 to 1938 and written by or ascribed to Mao described in great detail the application of these things in China and potentially in other backward countries. In *Basic Tactics, Strategic Problems of China's Revolutionary War, Strategic Problems of Anti-Japanese Guerrilla War, On Protracted War*, and *Problems of War and Strategy*, Mao outlined the tactics of guerrilla war and a strategy of waging from self-sufficient rural base areas both civil war and resistance to foreign occupation. It is important to note that Mao did not advocate—indeed he ridiculed—"pure" guerrilla warfare by lightly armed small groups with a constantly shifting locale. Rather, he envisaged the coordinated development and use of both guerrilla forces and a regular army, as well as the development of permanent territorial bases that if possible would be defended against attack. He envisaged the struggle against Japan as a "protracted war." Japan's stronger and more modern invading forces would win the initial battles; but in a long war of attrition a mobilized China, making use of its vast territory and interior position, would wear down the Japanese. Eventually the Chinese would be in a position to go on the offensive. In broad outlines this did not differ much from Jiang Jieshi's strategy, and neither Chinese faction was ever actually in a position to launch a decisive counteroffensive. But Mao's concept proved applicable in the civil war waged after World War II, and also in the First Indochina War.

In subsequent years Mao added a number of other major works on doctrine. In "On New Democracy" (1940) he outlined the form of regime the Communists planned to establish, a "joint dictatorship" of the revolutionary classes and parties, which under Communist leadership would conduct China's "bourgeois-democratic revolution"; only after that would a transition to socialism take place. Private ownership of the means of production would not be abolished immediately. In the early 1940s Mao launched a "rectification campaign" to "sinicize Marxism-Leninism" that was designed to secure his increased control of the party and was perhaps aimed at antagonists more closely associated with the Soviets than he was.[5]

The precise relations between Mao and the Chinese Communists and Moscow in the 1930s and 1940s are a rather murky business. The issue is complicated by various "revelations," especially from the Soviet side, which appear to be moves in the later Soviet-Chinese propaganda war rather than truthful accounts. It is certainly not the case, however, as is sometimes suggested in the West, that as early as the 1930s the Soviets and the Chinese Communists had little to do with each other or were even actively hostile. In fact, some of the most prominent Chinese Communist leaders, notably Zhou Enlai (Chou En-lai) and Lin Biao (Lin Piao) visited the Soviet Union for extended stays in the late 1930s and early 1940s. Mao, who never left China at all until 1949, was an outstanding exception, but even he sent one of his wives and his son to Moscow to obtain medical care and education. Although Mao's rise to power occurred at the expense of the Soviet-installed Returned Student faction, Moscow did not actively obstruct his career. In fact the Soviets do not seem to have intervened in the internal workings of the Chinese party after 1931. Nor does Mao seem to have openly defied Soviet policy, although on some occasions he followed Soviet orders only reluctantly and later was to give them an "interpretation" of his own. The Chinese Communists clearly remained a loyal element of the Soviet-directed Communist movement. They rigidly followed Soviet foreign policy, acclaiming the Nazi-Soviet Pact and the former Soviet-Japanese treaty of 1941 and every other move made by Stalin. Mao was not a spineless puppet such as headed most Western Communist parties. Neither was he a heretic.[6]

During 1937 and 1938 the Japanese advance opened the way for the expansion of the Chinese Communists. The Japanese quickly overran most of the developed areas of China and inflicted huge losses on the best Nationalist troops. Especially in the North, where the Guomindang had never been very strong in any case, the Japanese drove the Nationalist forces out of far more territory than they themselves could effectively control. Local government officials and many landlords fled with the retreating Nationalists. Most of the peasants might well have submitted to Japanese rule if the Japanese had behaved decently. But the Japanese advance was accompanied by an orgy of murder, rape, and looting.

The Communist forces entered this vast no-man's-land. Their regular forces pushed east into Shansi and inflicted a severe and well-publicized defeat on a Japanese division at Pingxing Guan (Pinghsingkwan) in September 1937, the first real tactical reverse suffered by the Japanese in China. The Communist regular units and special propaganda teams began organizing the population for guerrilla warfare, sometimes absorbing guerrilla groups organized by local leaders. Where possible they sought to create permanent "base areas" as opposed to "guerrilla areas" where irregular forces had to contest Japanese control directly. Since what happened in China has often been oversimplified as a "peasant revolution" that the Communists merely happened to take over, it should be noted that the Communists found it most useful to begin organizing local resistance not by contacting the peasants directly but by aiming their efforts initially at local students, handicraft workers, small businessmen, and such officials and landlords as remained and were reliably patriotic. Beginning with these relatively educated and aware elements, they brought the population into an assortment of "National Salvation Associations," each directed toward a specific membership of women, youth, certain occupations, and so on. The Communists then went on to form local "self-defense corps," stretcher units, and transportation units to support their military operations. The defeated Nationalist forces had left behind many weapons, which were the primary source for the expansion of the Communist forces. The Communists set up local "democratic" governments on the so-called three-thirds system. Only one-third of the government positions were allotted to Communists. Another third went to "progressive" individuals who were not actually members of the Communist party, and one-third to other groups. In practice, however, these governments were kept under effective Communist control. In some cases quite large forces under non-Communist leaders were operating in Japanese-occupied China; in these instances the Communists offered to fight alongside them under the united front policy. They then gradually infiltrated their ranks, undermining the older leaders over a long period. Finally they absorbed them. The Communist propaganda line was overwhelmingly devoted to patriotic and anti-Japanese themes, and the Communists' land policy was quite moderate. But the policy was well-calculated to win support for the party in the long run as well as for wartime purposes. The remaining "patriotic" landlords were left alone, whereas the land of real or alleged traitors and those who had fled was confiscated and redistributed. A moratorium was placed on debts; rents were lowered and interest rates limited. The chaotic and regressive land tax system was reorganized. The result of these measures was that in spite of the war many peasants were far better off than before, and thus they were inclined to identify their interests with those of the party. By 1940 there were 19 stable base areas behind the Japanese lines. The Communist Eighth Route Army controlled 400,000 troops and a population of 44 million people in North China alone. In central China a similar development based on small groups left behind on the Long March had produced a 100,000-man force, the New Fourth Army.[7]

By 1939 considerable friction had developed between the Communists and the Nationalists; the Communists were probably the more aggressive side. The Soviets had wanted Mao to adhere strictly to the united front policy and respect Nationalist leadership in the war against Japan. In late 1937 they flew Chen Shaoyu, who had been in Moscow since 1933, to the Communist capital of Yenan. With him were sent a load of radio equipment and weapons Mao probably found more welcome. While ordered to recognize Mao's control of the party, Chen was supposed to keep him aligned with the Nationalists. In practice, however, Mao gave a more aggressive interpretation to the united front, sanctioning armed clashes on a local basis and political activities against the Nationalists, confident that the latter could not afford to begin a full-scale civil war. The Nationalists retaliated by actions against the Communists and assembled troops along the border between the Nationalist area and the Shaanxi base area, instituting an economic blockade. In January 1941 a major clash, the New Fourth Army incident, marked the virtual breakdown of the united front.[8] It was apparent that all-out civil war would probably be resumed if and when the Japanese left.

In August 1940, perhaps in response to Soviet pressure at a time when Stalin was unnerved by the fall of France and wished to tie down Japan to prevent an early two-front attack on the Soviet Union, the Communists launched a major offensive against the Japanese. This stimulated the Japanese command into finally taking the Communists seriously. In July 1941 the Japanese launched a campaign of incredible ferocity against the Communists in the north. This "three-all" campaign—"kill all, burn all, destroy all"— cut the Communist forces from 400,000 down to 300,000 men and cut the population under their control nearly in half. The brutal antiguerrilla effort, however, could not be continued. During 1942 and 1943 the growing U.S. threat in the Pacific caused the Japanese to transfer seven first-class infantry divisions from China, leaving their forces there too weak to finish off the Communists. The savagery of the three-all campaign had left hardly an intact village in North China, and the brutalities of the Japanese had welded the peasants more tightly to the Communists. In collaboration with the puppet government set up under Wang Jingwei in 1940, the Japanese did attempt a more humane counterguerrilla effort in central China. This "Rural Pacification Movement," which used the Japanese only to fight armed guerrillas, was launched in July

1941 on a small scale. It left administration in Chinese hands and instituted some reforms. Although it had some success in pacifying several areas near the Chang Jiang mouth, it was too little and too late. For by the time the movement was well underway, it was clear that Japan would lose the war. Outside of the few "Model Peace Zones" produced by this campaign, the Communists soon recovered their strength.[9] They had succeeded in building the base of power from which they were to conquer all of China.

The Era of the Nazi-Soviet Pact

The Nazi-Soviet Pact was probably not, as was often later claimed, the "trigger" for World War II. Hitler was reckless enough to attack Poland even without a clear-cut agreement neutralizing the Soviet Union. However, the arrangements between Germany and the Soviet Union, which made the Soviets a nonbelligerent ally of Germany, did provide substantial help to the Nazis and formed the background to Germany's victories in the first years of the war. Although the pact was only a distateful, short-term expedient from Hitler's point of view, it was a major strategic move for Stalin. For him it was the realization of the hopes outlined in 1925; the major powers of the capitalist world were set at each other's throats, while the Soviet Union was able to conserve its strength. The war broke the confines to which the Soviets had been subjected since 1921. The areas of Eastern Europe consigned to the Soviets by the secret protocol were probably seen as just the first gains to be reaped from the pact.

On September 17, after it became apparent that the Germans had defeated the Poles, the Red Army marched into eastern Poland. That area was simply annexed to the Belorussian and Ukrainian Soviet Republics and brutally assimilated. Between a million and a million and a half people, mostly members of the Polish minority in the annexed areas, were deported to Soviet labor camps. The

Baltic countries were approached more gradually. In later September and early October the Soviets demanded that these countries sign "mutual assistance pacts" granting the Soviets military bases. There was no prospect of help from the outside; Stalin issued effusive assurances that the Soviets would not interfere in the Baltic States' internal affairs. They submitted.[1] On September 28 a Soviet-German joint declaration urged Britain and France to make peace with Germany.

The Communist parties in the West were somewhat bewildered by the Nazi-Soviet Pact and subsequent events. The Soviets were probably deliberately slow about changing the "line" of the Communist movement. At first the British and French Communists continued to take a "patriotic" line. The French Communists voted for war credits, and their leaders joined the army when the reserves were called up. When the Red Army crossed the Polish frontier, they were finally ordered to change their tune. The Soviets and their followers denounced the struggle between Germany and the Allies as an "imperialist war" and took up a stance superficially similar to the policy of "revolutionary defeatism" followed by Lenin during World War I. At first they seemed to condemn both sides equally. However, with the Western powers' rejection of the Soviet-German call for peace, the Soviets had an excuse to blame the democracies for the war. The switch from "antifascism" to effective support for Nazism was sufficiently violent to make even some hardened Stalinists sick. Indeed, the French Communist leader Maurice Thorez may have seriously considered breaking with Moscow. But he did not do so; and although losing much support and many members, the world's Communist parties survived basically intact.[2]

The pro-German line became more and more extreme. The Communists in German-occupied countries opposed resistance and opposed the attempts of the governments-in-exile to carry on the war. A special Comintern publication in German, "Die Welt," was particularly extreme. It was openly pro-German and sometimes used quasi-Nazi and anti-Semitic themes. By February 1940 the German Communist leader Walter Ulbricht was calling in its pages for the German workers to support the Nazi regime against Britain. Meanwhile, Communists in the West did their best to spread defeatism. During 1940 French Communists sabotaged tank and aircraft plants, and Czech Communists managed to launch a mutiny in the Czech armed forces in exile.[3] As the pro-Nazi line became more extreme, the Western powers and the Soviets drifted in the direction of war. The Soviets opened a naval base near Murmansk for the use of the Germans. Soviet supplies and the transit trade from East Asia over the Trans-Siberian railroad were a tremendous help to Germany; fuel and rubber supplies were particularly valuable. In early 1940 the Soviet icebreakers helped a German raider, the *Komet*, reach the Pacific by the Northeast Passage.[4]

On October 12, 1939, the Soviets confronted the Finnish government with a series of demands similar to those given to the Baltic States. Finland was to allow the construction of a Soviet base and cede a considerable slice of territory on the Karelian isthmus, which would serve to place Leningrad out of range of artillery fire from Finnish territory. In return Stalin offered to trade a large but desolate area of Soviet Karelia. The Finns offered to give up some territory but felt that any more concessions would be suicidal. Unlike the Baltic countries, they felt able to resist.

Stalin does not appear to have been too displeased. An invasion was hastily, and poorly, planned and prepared with the aim of conquering the whole country. Stalin seems to have assumed that the illegal Finnish Communist party was basically strong and that the Finnish government would quickly collapse under attack. Marshal Shaposhnikov, the sober chief of the general staff, had prepared a sensible plan assuming that the Finns would put up a stiff fight. Stalin rejected it and ordered the Leningrad Military District to prepare a more optimistic scheme. The war was expected to last only 10 to 20 days.

On November 30 a massive Soviet force of 600,000 men attacked without a declaration of war. The main blow was a direct thrust straight up the Karelian isthmus; it was accompanied by a series of dispersed secondary attacks north of Lake Ladoga. But the expectations of a Finnish collapse proved unfounded. The Finnish people were completely loyal to their government, and the Finnish Communist government set up at Terijoki on the frontier was a complete failure. Even Finnish Communists ignored it. Despite its small size Finland, ably led by Mannerheim, was well-prepared for war while the Soviets were not. The Red Army even seems to have been unprepared for winter, and both the army and air force units employed in Finland proved poorly trained. The Soviet infantry had not been trained in forest fighting, and cooperation between the various arms was poor. The Finns learned how to separate Soviet armor from its accompanying infantry; they simply tricked the tanks into traps or set them on fire with "Molotov cocktails." Ski-equipped Finnish units proved much more mobile than the Red Army. They outflanked the Soviet thrusts north of Lake Ladoga and encircled many units.

World opinion and the Nazi leaders drew rather exaggerated conclusions from the initial Soviet defeats in Finland. (The brillant Soviet victory at Khalkin Ghol was practically unknown.) The Soviet Union was widely believed to be a weak and incompetent giant. The Western countries were deeply sympathetic to the Finns; the British allowed arms and even individual British volunteers to go to Finland.

Many people wished to go further. They believed that the Russo-Finnish War had opened an important strategic opportunity. Germany was then dependent on shipments of iron ore from northern Sweden, which during part of the year was shipped via the Norwegian port of Narvik and Norwegian coastal waters to Germany. During early 1940 the Allies developed a scheme designed to help the Finns and deny Germany iron ore. It was planned to land at Narvik a force of up to 57,000 men, nominally "volunteers." Part of this force would move to support the Finns, but most would secure control over the Swedish orefields. The volunteer status of the force would, it was hoped, help avert outright war with the Soviet Union. The plan was blocked by Allied unreadiness and the simple refusal of the Norwegian and Swedish governments to go along, yet it was under intense discussion right up to the end of the Russo-Finnish War, as were other measures. The British had no desire for all-out war with the Soviet Union; the French, however, were more reckless. The French government maintained that, for all practical purposes, the Soviet Union was already an ally of Germany and at war with Britain and France—a view which was greatly exaggerated, but certainly not unfounded— and that there was no reason for the Western powers to be cautious. Some of the French on the extreme right actively favored outright war with the Soviets for a different reason; they hoped that an opportunity would then arise to make peace with Germany. The French government proposed not only sending troops to Finland but blockading Soviet ports on the Black Sea and bombing Baku, the main center of Soviet oil production. The British moved cautiously but agreed that there was some chance of war with the Soviet Union. They established contact with Caucasian and Central Asian nationalist movements and prepared for an air offensive against Baku. A British reconnaissance plane flew over Baku and Batum at the end of March. By that time, however, the Finnish war was over.

In January the Soviets hastily began diplomatic moves to placate the Western powers and laid plans to bring the war to a conclusion. Although Stalin concluded a major new trade agreement with Germany on February 11, its implementation was delayed. Meanwhile, the Red Army on the Finnish front was reinforced and reorganized. In early February, under a crushing weight of artillery fire, the Soviets broke through the Finnish defenses on the Karelian isthmus. The heroic resistance of the Finns, and Stalin's fear of a war with the Western powers, caused the Soviets to settle for the bare territorial demands they had made in the fall of 1939. Peace was concluded on March 12. The Terijoki regime simply vanished.[5] Stalin still feared British and French action. He did not breathe more easily until the German invasion of Norway and Denmark on April 9. Molotov then wished Germany "complete success" in her "defensive measures."

In May 1940 the pro-German line reached its peak, but Stalin's policy then suffered a disastrous collapse with the defeat of France and the German conquest of Western Eruope. Although the magnitude of the German victories were not only unexpected but certainly unwelcome, the Soviets and their supporters tried to exploit them. Stalin seems to have hoped that Hitler would reward his pro-German stand by letting the local Communists have a role in running the occupied areas. The new move began in Norway. After the German invasion the Norwegian Communists asked the German command for preferential treatment and control over the labor movement. The Germans agreed to this. Then the Communists proposed eliminating the old Norwegian constitution and forming a new government backed by the labor organization they now controlled. The Germans balked at this and then suppressed the Communists. In Denmark, France, and Belgium the Communists approached the Germans in a similar way. As preliminary moves they asked for the legalization of their party, the release of imprisoned Communists, and the right to publish newspapers. In return they offered to make peace with Germany and support the German war effort. The Nazis rejected these overtures.[6]

Stalin made a direct and somewhat more effective response in the sphere under his control. The Soviets took over the Baltic States in a process whose first stages resembled a rushed and crude version of the takeovers of Mongolia, Eastern Europe, and North Korea, although Soviet personnel played an even bigger and more brutal role. In late May the Soviets reinforced the units stationed on their bases in Lithuania. They began to stage "incidents" between the Soviet troops and the Baltic countries, which were accused of "anti-Soviet" acts. On June 15 an ultimatum was delivered to the Lithuanian government: It was to allow more Soviet forces in or else. The Red Army crossed the frontier even before the Lithuanians could surrender. Two days later Estonia and Latvia received the same treatment. The Soviets then appointed puppet prime ministers in the three countries to replace the legitimate leaders; in Estonia this act was accompanied by a farcical "uprising" staged by the tiny local Communist party. The Communists of the three Baltic countries each formed a front organization called the "Union of Working People." In fake elections on

July 14–15 these groups "won" an overwhelming mandate. The resulting "parliaments" then voted to admit themselves to the Soviet Union. The Baltic peoples were treated exceptionally badly; by the time of the Nazi invasion in 1941, 2 percent of their populations had been deported to Soviet prisons and concentration camps.

In a parallel move Stalin forced Romania to cede Bessarabia. He had pushed the Soviet frontier far to the west, but the territories gained in 1939–40 proved of little defensive value to the Soviet Union, and they drove the Romanians and the Baltic peoples, previously pro-Allied in sentiment, straight into the arms of Germany.[7]

After the fall of France Stalin was finally genuinely frightened of Germany—and with good reason, for Hitler was resolved to attack the Soviet Union at the earliest possible moment. Only on June 26, 1940, did Stalin formally put Soviet industry on a war basis. The movement of workers was frozen and the hours of work lengthened. In the futile hope of placating Hitler, Stalin continued a strongly pro-German foreign policy. The British, De Gaulle, and the governments-in-exile were strongly condemned for continuing the war.

As it became clear in the late summer and fall of 1940 that Britain would not be defeated quickly, Stalin's nerves recovered somewhat. He was convinced, or convinced himself, that Germany was still tied down by Britain's resistance and must focus on beating the British in the near future. Dependent on imports from the Soviet Union, Hitler would not attack the Soviet Union. However, Stalin found that despite the terms of the Nazi-Soviet Pact, Germany was blocking Soviet moves in the sphere he had been assigned. German troops had moved, as yet in small numbers, into Romania and Finland, and a number of lesser irritants had caused friction between the two totalitarian powers. The Nazis invited Foreign Minister Molotov to a conference at Berlin beginning on November 12, purportedly to coordinate the long-range policies of the Soviets and the Axis powers (Germany, Italy, and Japan had recently signed their formal alliance, the Tripartite Pact, aimed at the English-speaking countries).

At the November meeting the Nazis energetically tried to align the Soviets with the Axis powers and to push the Soviets into expanding south into the British-dominated Middle East. Hitler's foreign minister, Joachim von Ribbentrop, was unenthusiastic about an attack on the Soviets and may have wanted a real alliance. Hitler himself probably hoped merely to divert Soviet forces and make his attack on them easier, perhaps thus setting the stage for peace with Britain. Molotov refused to be drawn in, however, and instead focused on matters relating to the Soviets' immediate neighbors in Europe. Neither side made concessions on these things. But Stalin's objections to becoming a full if nonbelligerent partner of the Axis were a matter of price, not principle. On November 25 the Soviets offered to join in a four-power pact—in effect to join the Tripartite Pact—on the conditions that the Germans withdraw from Finland, that Bulgaria sign a mutual-assistance pact with the Soviet Union, in effect making that country a Soviet satellite, that the Soviets secure a naval and military base in Turkey near the straits, that Soviet rights to expand in the area "south of Batum and Baku" (e.g., Iran), be recognized and that Japan renounce her right to oil and coal concessions in Soveit Sakhalin. The Nazis did not bother to reply.[8] In March 1941 German, not Soviet forces, entered Bulgaria in preparation for the attack on Greece and Yugoslavia.

At the beginning of April Stalin tried indecisively to bolster Yugoslavia's resistance to a German attack, making gestures of friendship and signing a nonaggression pact. The pact had hardly been signed, however, when Yugoslavia was overrun by the Germans. Shortly afterward the Soviets secretly alerted their forces on the Belorussian frontier and began transferring some troops from the Soviet Far East to the west. On April 13, 1941, Stalin managed to arrange a "Neutrality Pact" with Japan. The Soviets tacitly recognized Japanese control of Manchuria in return for Japan's recognition of Outer Mongolia. This was the last prewar diplomatic triumph for the Soviets. They had succeeded in discouraging Japan from joining in a German attack on the Soviet Union, steering the Japanese southward instead. But then a panicky Stalin seems to have retreated into a fixed refusal to believe the rapidly accumulating evidence of a German attack. No further preparations or even coherent plans were made for war. In May, in a last spasm of appeasement the Soviets broke diplomatic relations with the governments-in-exile of Belgium, Norway, and Yugo-slavia and recognized the pro-Axis government that had briefly seized power in Iraq.[9] It was all useless. On June 22, 1941, the German armies roared into the Soviet Union. For the next year and a half the Soviets and the world Communist movement were engaged in a desperate struggle for survival. Much against his will Stalin had been forced into an alliance with the Western democracies. However, Stalin had still not quite absorbed the true antifascist spirit, for even after World War II he nostalgically referred to the Nazi-Soviet Pact, "Ech, together with the Germans, we would have been invincible."[10]

In 1941 it seemed to many that Soviet foreign policies and the Soviet-controlled Communist movement had simply been a failure. There had been no successful Communist revolutions since 1917, except for the "revolution from the outside" in Mongolia. The Soviet Union had had little success at expansion, except in an alliance with Nazi Germany—an alliance that had backfired disastrously. Whether or not the Soviet Union survived the Nazi attack—and most Westerners did not expect it to survive—it appeared that little had been achieved.

This, however, was a superficial view. Disappointing as developments had been in comparison with the high hopes of 1917, a very real basis had been laid for future victories. The industrialization drive and the buildup of the Red Army had, despite all the follies of Stalin's policies and the Great Purges, made the Soviet Union one of the world's most powerful countries. Part of its new industrial development, the Urals-Kuznetsk combine, was securely located far from attack. The Soviet Union had drawn even with or ahead of Germany in most of the quantitative indices of industrial production, although the general quality of Soviet industrial products was inferior to those of the "capitalist world." Even that criticism did not apply, however, to the appliances most prized by the Soviet leaders, the weapons of their armed forces. The Red

Army and Red Air Force had been built up to a great force of more than 4 million men, with as many planes and more tanks than the rest of the world combined. Because of overproduction earlier, and perhaps a rigidity induced by the Great Purges, most of these machines were obsolete. But new fighters and dive-bombers were coming off the assembly lines that would approach the performance of their Western counterparts. At the time of the German invasion, nearly 1,500 new T-34 and KV tanks, better than anything the Germans or anybody else had, had been delivered. The Soviets were far ahead of the rest of the world in tank design and the development of rocket artillery, and their cannon and small arms were as good as or better than those of the other great powers. Although its morale was shaky in 1941 and it suffered from tactical rigidity and a lack of initiative among its junior officers, the Red Army was a formidable force. Russians, and at least some of the subject nationalities, were sturdy soldiers renowned for their resilience under bombardment, their stolidity in miserable conditions, and their stubbornness in defense. Contrary to what was generally thought in 1941, the Red Army would prove effective both in defense and expansion.

Beyond the Soviet frontiers the foundations of a Communist regime had been laid in China. If Communists elsewhere had not been very successful, they had been forged into disciplined instruments of Soviet power, and most of them would stay that way until the break between the Soviet Union and Communist China in the 1960s. Between the efforts of the NKVD (Soviet secret police) and local Communist parties, the Soviet Union was the best-informed government in the world, and it had a unique ability to intervene in the internal politics of many other countries.

Many of the devices and techniques successfully used by the Soviet state during the cold war had already been tried, albeit often unsuccessfully, on a small scale and in relatively out of the way and unimportant places in the era between the world wars. The techniques of building a satellite state, the use of proxy forces or volunteers under Soviet control to influence the outcome of revolutions and civil wars, were already seen in the 1920s and 1930s. So was the judicious use of Soviet military aid supported by the inconspicuous employment of Soviet advisors and airmen in civil and international struggles. The basic strategies and tactics of the world's Communist parties were largely perfected in this era, even if their application was not too successful. (In fact, it is doubtful if Communists have ever been able to devise anything but modest variations and extensions of the ideas that sprang from Lenin's nimble brain.) The 1920s and 1930s saw the Communists develop the logical implications of Lenin's emphasis on elitism and guiding the masses and deception. The remnants of the influences of social democracy and Marxist theory were eliminated. The Communists shifted their emphasis from the actions of the "masses" and aiming at purportedly popular uprisings to the greater use of manipulation and the use of coups and military forces, from overt political movements to the use of infiltration. They shifted from their original insistence on a "proletarian" base of support and the use of overtly Marxist-Leninist terminology to the use of other classes (peasants or some subdivision of the "bourgeoisie") and the use of pseudo-democratic or liberal phraseology. In the era between the wars the Soviets and their followers also encountered what was to become a perennial problem; the difficulty of dealing with nationalist movements in the underdeveloped countries. Even the development of "national communism" can be seen as early as the 1920s, although "National Communists" were no more successful than the Muscovite brand.

Diversionary Formulas

Mundus Vult Decipi (The world wishes to be deceived).
—Petronius

The era between the world wars saw more than the development of various political techniques by the Soviets. It also saw Westerners develop various techniques to help evade the realities of the Soviet Union and the Communist movement, what James Burnham once called "diversionary formulas."[1] These formulas served to minimize the dangers presented by the Soviets and their followers in other countries. They belittled the strength of the Soviet Union, or attributed excessively benign intentions to the Soviet leaders, or comforted Western democrats with the notion that the Soviets were changing their doctrine or behavior. Many of these formulas have persisted in modified form right up to the present, and they are worth examining at some length.

It is perhaps necessary to note here that the author does not wish to suggest that there has never been any possibility of the Soviet regime evolving in a moderate direction or, on the other hand, that it can never meet with economic disaster. But during the period between the world wars and periodically during the cold war, Westerners often imagined that the Soviet Union was already undergoing desirable changes or was on the verge of collapse when there was no real sign that either of these things was taking place. The purpose of this chapter is to examine these illusions.

Many people held that the Soviet Union was basically weak and that communism was necessarily ineffective because it was "against human nature." Notions of this sort were quite popular among people of moderate political views. On the far right they tended to shade into an odd conception of Communist rule as a sort of infectious chaos rather than as a highly organized modern tyranny. Often such views stemmed from the belief that capitalism corresponded to human nature and was the "natural" social order, a notion that was the product of limited knowledge and imagination; far from being "natural," capitalism is a comparatively recent development. Collectivist economies have perhaps been historically more common than those based on private ownership. Many argued that a Communist society could not be a danger because of its economic inefficiency. The phrase "communism does not work" still recurs in Western commentary on Soviet affairs. But, while there are excellent reasons to believe that Communist economies are less productive than capitalist or mixed economies, the Soviets nevertheless managed to modernize their country. Despite the terrible inadequacy of Soviet farming the economy functioned, even if it continued to trail behind that of the most advanced countries.

Another reason for complacency may have been the belief that the Russians were a nation of bunglers, a belief apparently derived from an exaggerated emphasis on the underdevelopment of Imperial Russia and a one-eyed view of the Russian performance in World War I. This notion appeared as late as the 1950s, when the Soviets' development of the atomic bomb was attributed solely to the successes of Soviet espionage; and their development of intercontinental missiles and satellites, to the help of captured German scientists. (In fact it was the Americans who had acquired most of the German scientists.) There are, perhaps, revealing similarities between this type of thinking about the U.S.S.R. and U.S. attitudes toward Japan before World War II. As described by Edwin Reischauer, "it is disconcerting to note that deteriorating relations between the United States and Japan produced an increasingly ostrich-like attitude on the part of Americans. The more Japanese and American interests clashed and the more acute the disagreements between our two lands became, the more deeply and carefully we should have studied Japan and the Japanese, if not in an effort to understand them, at least in an effort to thwart them. Instead, we chose to ignore them, to attempt to make Japan insignificant by refusing to recognize its importance to us. Our reaction was basically emotional rather than rational. Instead of facing our problems realistically, we were almost like a primitive people attempting to vanquish their foes by sympathetic magic." Instead of recognizing that Japan was an advanced industrial country and a formidable foe, Americans compulsively belittled the Japanese and underestimated Japan's strength.[2] Although Western attitudes toward the Soviets since 1917 have been more ambiguous and complex than the U.S. attitude toward the Japanese before Pearl Harbor, mental aberrations of the sort dissected by Reischauer have not been absent from them. Like Japan, the Soviet Union was a late-comer to the industrial world; if not really "non-Western," it too stood outside familiar patterns. In many people's minds it should not really have been there; or, at least, it could not count for much.

A more defensible variant of the belief in Soviet weakness was the conviction that the crimes of the regime were so great that it had permanently alienated much of the population. Perhaps at its root lay the simple conviction that any regime so evil simply could not last. In the era between the world wars many people, especially in the English-speaking countries, were still sure that right would triumph in the end. It is a conviction that seems to have died out in the last generation or so.

Even sober commentators could, however, find good reason for thinking like this before the Soviet-German war. The American ambassador, Laurence Steinhardt, believed in 1941 that the Ukrainians and the Russian peasants hated the regime so much that the mere arrival of the German army would topple it. This view was by no means unfounded, for many Russians, as well as members of other nationalities, did defect during the war. But Steinhardt and others like him underestimated the strengths of a totalitarian regime and the degree to which even notoriously incompetent, unjust, and evil governments can appeal to patriotism. There was no organized opposition to the Soviet regime. Terror, effective organization, and all-embracing propaganda did not necessarily inspire enthusiasm for the regime, but reduced the people to an inert, apathetic mass who were often unable to imagine something better.[3]

At the opposite political and moral pole from the conviction that the Soviet regime was just too evil to last lay the beliefs of Soviet sympathizers in the West. These ranged from essential acceptance of the Communist claim to be creating paradise in the "socialist sixth of the world," a belief enshrined in Sidney and Beatrice Webb's *Soviet Communism*, to the view that although short of perfection (often faults were blamed on "Russian backwardness"), the U.S.S.R. nevertheless represented a "progressive" social order and therefore opposition to the Soviet Union and communism was inherently and inevitably "reactionary." For a proponent of the latter view there were no enemies on the left, except perhaps liberals and socialists who were strongly anticommunist, and whom they often hated more than those farther to the right.

With little apparent justification Soviet sympathizers often projected their own obsessions, dreams, and fears onto the Soviet regime. Egalitarians decided that Soviet society must be a splendid example of economic equality at a time when it was characterized by greater differentials of income than the West and when the aim of equalizing income had been explicitly repudiated by Stalin as "petty-bourgeois." Others professed to see the Soviet Union as an example of sexual freedom when in fact it was more conservative in such matters than the West. Jewish sympathizers with the Soviets professed to believe that anti-Semitism had been wiped out in the Soviet Union.

The belief that the Soviet Union represented "progress" and humanitarianism and the cause of antifascism was, of course, especially attractive in the bleak period of the Great Depression and during the rise of Hitler. Yet the attraction of the Soviet Union and communism, for there was still no real distinction between the two, reached its peak during the most brutal phase of the Soviet regime; and this was no accident either. Some Westerners were attracted to Soviet totalitarianism precisely because of its murderous and tyrannical nature. Bertolt Brecht may have been an example of this; in defending Stalin's purges he told Sydney Hook, "The more innocent they are, the more they deserve to die." The influential pro-Soviet journalist Walter Duranty dismissed the sufferings of the Soviet population with sadistic contempt, declaring that Stalin's victims were "only Russians." He carefully failed to mention their sufferings in his reports. In another mood he assured the West that Stalin was "making men out of mice." (The effectiveness and broad nature of the Soviets' appeal in this era is shown by its remarkable ability to enlist in its services the support of both misguided humanitarians and the morally callous.) To disarm their critics morally and provide a refuge for their more soft-hearted counterparts, the more extreme Soviet sympathizers devised what George Orwell wittily called the "theory of catastrophic gradualism." As Orwell put it, this theory maintained that "nothing is ever achieved without bloodshed, lies, tyranny and injustice, but on the other hand no considerable change for the better is to be expected as the result of even the greatest upheaval." He summarized its implications by observing that "if you object to dictatorship you are a reactionary but if you expect dictatorship to produce results you are a sentimentalist."[4] "Catastrophic gradualism" proved the twentieth-century substitute for patriotism as the last refuge of a scoundrel.

More moderate sympathizers helped to create the myth that the Soviets and the world's Communist parties had abandoned expansion and world revolution. Wrenching Stalin's phrase out of context, they claimed that the Soviets were interested only in "socialism in one country." The impression was even created, partly by manipulating reactions to Nazi propaganda, that communism had never been an aggressive, revolutionary force. Arthur Koestler, who worked for the Comintern in the 1930s, credited this feat to the Communists themselves. He later wrote of their "achievement in effacing from public memory the fact that for years, in Germany and elsewhere, they had preached violence and armed rebellion. The evidence was there—on the front page of every Communist paper. But as the [Reichstag Fire] Trial had established that they had not planned an armed rebellion on the day of the fire of the Reichstag the public regarded it as implicitly proved that they never had and never would at any date."[5]

Various groups with little or no affection for the Soviet regime or communism also contributed their share of diversionary formulas designed to explain that the Soviets or their followers were not a real danger. One idea influential between the wars was popularized by Nicholas Berdyaev and other Russian émigré intellectuals. They held that the development of communism stemmed from Russia's unique religious heritage and some other peculiar national characteristics. It was a product, although also a horrible distortion, of Russian tradition. While perhaps not ruling out Soviet imperial expansion, this school of thought tended to hold that other countries would remain naturally immune to communism.[6] But these ideas proved clearly untenable after World War II, when Communist revolutions occurred in countries as diverse as China, Cuba, Vietnam, and Ethiopia, often against much less bitter resistance than the Bolsheviks had had to face from their Russian opponents. Russia's unusual political and economic situation had indeed been indispensable as the starting point for the world Communist movement. A Leninist-type revolution was unlikely to succeed in a country more advanced than tsarist Russia, while Lenin's doctrine could not have originated in a truly backward land. But Leninism could be introduced and implemented in underdeveloped countries, even if it could not have originated there. The experience of other countries, too, showed that the horrors of Soviet rule were not due to some unique Russian capacity for tyranny or evil. Some later Communist regimes, notably those in Albania, North Korea, and Cambodia, proved even more tyrannical and murderous than Stalin's regime at its worst.

Theories of more lasting popularity explained that some overwhelming force or tendency beyond its control would ultimately render the Soviet regime innocuous. Most prominent was the "convergence" theory first expounded by the well-known Austrian socialist theoretician Otto Bauer in his book *Kapitalismus und Sozialismus nach dem Kriege* in 1931. Bauer held that two parallel processes of socialization were taking place in Europe, one via democratic socialism in the West, the other via socialist tyranny in the Soviet Union. Patience and mutual tolerance would bridge the gap between the two forms. Neither trend could be eliminated by the other; meanwhile socialists should try to work with the Soviets. In a few years, as its economy grew, Soviet living standards would improve, and the regime would gradually evolve toward democracy. Bauer's errors were scathingly exposed by Russian socialist émigrés; nonetheless, especially when stripped of its specifically socialist form of sentimentality, his theory proved lastingly popular. It has been revived again and again in various forms during and right after the second world war by the Russian emigrés Pitirim Sorokin and N. S. Timasheff, and in the 1960s by John Kenneth Galbraith. Often closely related to the convergence theory were views that an allegedly inevitable postrevolutionary trend toward normalization must force the Soviet regime to become more moderate, or that the reopening or increase of trade contacts with the West would cause it either to return to capitalism or otherwise become reasonable. Illusions of this sort, traceable to nineteenth-century liberalism, appeared at an early date. In February 1920 the British prime minister, Lloyd George, declared, "We have failed to restore Russia to sanity by force. I believe we can save her by trade. Commerce has a sobering influence.... Trade, in my opinion, will bring an end to the ferocity, the rapine and the crudity of Bolshevism surer than any other method." In May 1921 Lady Kennet recorded in her diary that "[Fridjhof] Nansen was here to tea and gave me the reassuring news that our troubles with Russia are over. Lenin is introducing a New Economic Policy which restores a free market and represents a return to capitalist exchange of goods in Russia." Later in 1921 Otto Bauer jeered that the Soviets were "retreating to capitalism." Lenin was sufficiently annoyed to reply that if Bauer had said that in Russia, he would have had him shot.[7] This remark, unfortunately, proved a better indicator of the basic characteristics of the Soviet regime than the NEP.

Such illusions served not only for the era between the world wars but for the cold war as well. In the last sixty years it has been difficult for those of an optimistic turn of mind to improve much upon Otto Bauer or Lloyd George.

Notes

CHAPTER 1: MARXISM AND LENINISM

1. Sidney Hook, *Marx and the Marxists* (Princeton: D. Van Nostrand,1955); Robert Tucker, *The Marxian Revolutionary Idea* (New York: Norton, 1969); R. N. Carew-Hunt, *The Theory and Practice of Communism* (Baltimore: Penguin, 1957), offer excellent introductions to Marx's ideas from varying points of view. The neglected issue of Marx's racial views is discussed in Saul Padover, *Karl Marx* (New York: McGraw-Hill, 1978), pp. 168–71, 326–27, 487, 499–500, 502; Leon Poliakov, *The Aryan Myth* (New York: New American Library, 1977), pp. 244–47.

2. Carew-Hunt, *The Theory and Practice of Communism*, pp. 159–212; Philip Selznick, *The Organizational Weapon*, (Glencoe: Free Press, 1960); Stanley Page, *Lenin and World Revolution* (New York: McGraw-Hill, 1972), pp. 1–23, 141–42; E. H. Carr, *The Bolshevik Revolution*, Vol. 1 (Baltimore: Penguin, 1970), pp. 15–79; Donald Treadgold, *Lenin and His Rivals* (New York: Praeger, 1955). Leonard Schapiro, *The Communist Party of the Soviet Union* (New York: Vintage, 1969), pp. 1–157; Adam Ulam, *The Bolsheviks* (New York: Collier, 1968), is the best biography of Lenin. See also Bertram Wolfe, *Three Who Made a Revolution* (New York: Dial, 1948). A good selection of Lenin's works can be found in *The Lenin Reader*, ed. Stefan Possony (Chicago: Regnery, 1966).

3. Cf. Walt W. Rostow, *Stages of Economic Growth* (Cambridge: Cambridge University Press, 1960), p. 110; D. K. Fieldhouse, *The Colonial Empires* (New York: Delacorte, 1966); D. K. Fieldhouse, *Economics and Empire* (Ithaca: Cornell University Press, 1973); Correlli Barnett, *The Collapse of British Power* (New York: Morrow, 1972); L. H. Gann and Peter Duignan, *Burden of Empire*

(Stanford: Hoover Institution Press, 1967); William Langer, *The Diplomacy of Imperialism* (Cambridge, MA: Harvard University Press, 1935).

4. E. H. Carr, *The Bolshevik Revolution*, Vol. 3 (Baltimore: Penguin, 1970), pp. 15–21, 541–60; Stefan Possony, *A Century of Conflict* (Chicago: Regnery, 1953); Lenin, *Sochineniya*, Vol. 18 (Moscow: 1930–35), pp. 232–33, 313; ibid., Vol. 19, pp. 323–25.

CHAPTER 2: THE RUSSIAN EMPIRE AND THE REVOLUTIONS OF 1917

1. W. H. Chamberlin, *The Russian Revolution*, Vol. 1 (New York: Grosset & Dunlap, 1965), pp. 1–62; ibid., Vol. 2, pp. 452–59; Michael Florinsky, *The End of the Russian Empire* (New York: Collier, 1961); Richard Charques, *The Twilight of Imperial Russia* (Oxford: Oxford University Press, 1958); Hugh Seton-Watson, *The Russian Empire* (New York: Praeger, 1967); *The Modernization of Russia and Japan*, ed. Cyril Black (New York: Free Press, 1975).

2. Chamberlin, *The Russian Revolution*, Vol. 1, pp. 63–64.

3. Norman Stone, *The Eastern Front* (New York: Scribner's, 1975); Winston Churchill, *The Unknown War* (New York: Scribner's, 1931).

4. Chamberlin, *The Russian Revolution*, Vol. 1, pp. 63–97; John Keep, *The Russian Revolution* (New York: Norton, 1976), pp. 57–62; Charques, *The Twilight of Imperial Russia*, pp. 236–44.

5. Chamberlin, *The Russian Revolution*, Vol 1, pp. 100–119, 142–276; Keep, *The Russian Revolution*, pp. 57–253; Stone, *The Eastern Front*, pp. 300–301; Possony, *A Century of Conflict*, pp. 29–59; Z.A.B. Zeman, *Germany and the Russian Revolution* (Oxford: Oxford University Press, 1958). For a different interpretation of Lenin's policy, see Page, *Lenin and World Revolution*, pp. 23–77.

6. S. P. Melgunov, *The Bolshevik Seizure of Power*, abridged and ed. S.G. and Boris Pushkarev (Santa Barbara, Calif.: ABC Books, 1972); Robert V. Daniels, *Red October* (New York: Scribner's, 1976); Chamberlin, *The Russian Revolution*, Vol. 1, pp. 277–350; Possony, *A Century of Conflict*, pp. 59–75.

7. Chamberlin, *The Russian Revolution*, Vol 1, pp. 348–49; Richard Pipes, *The Formation of the Soviet Union*, rev. ed. (Cambridge: Harvard University Press, 1964), pp. 50–72, 111–22; Alexandre Bennigsen, "The Conquest of the Moslem Borderlands," in *The Anatomy of Communist Takeovers*, ed. Thomas T. Hammond (New Haven: Yale University Press,1975), pp. 61–64; Carr, *The Bolshevik Revolution*, Vol. 1, pp. 259–91, 295–303, 423–33.

8. Chamberlin, *The Russian Revolution*, Vol. 1, pp. 351–72, 472–77, 479–89; Carr, *The Bolshevik Revolution*, Vol. 1, pp. 115–33, 160–61; Carr, *The Bolshevik Revolution*, Vol. 3, pp. 21–23, 29, 235–36.

9. Richard H. Ullman, *Intervention and the War* (Pinceton: Princeton University Press, 1961), pp. 3, 19, 29, 31; George F. Kennan, *Russia and the West under Lenin and Stalin* (New York: New American Library, 1962), pp. 37–48; Keep, *The Russian Revolution*, p. 252.

CHAPTER 3: CIVIL WAR AND INTERVENTION

1. Chamberlin, *The Russian Revolution*, Vol. 1, pp. 372–86; Pipes, *The Formation of the Soviet Union*, pp. 125–32; Peter Kenez, *Civil War in South Russia, 1918* (Berkeley: University of California Press, 1971), pp. 35–102; Sergei Starikov and Roy Medvedev, *Philip Mironov and the Russian Civil War* (New York: Knopf, 1978), pp. 4–12, 36–53; Ullman, *Intervention and the War* pp. 42, 47–48.

2. Chamberlin, *The Russian Revolution*, Vol. 1, pp. 390–412; Oleh Fedyshyn, *Germany's Drive to the East and the Ukrainian Revolution* (New Brunswick: Rutgers University Press, 1971), pp. 59–96.

3. Kenez, *Civil War in South Russia, 1918*, pp. 118–78; Starikov and Medvedev, *Philip Mironov*, pp. 58–68; Dimitri V. Lehovich, *White against Red* (New York: Norton, 1974), pp. 176–210.

4. Chamberlin, *The Russian Revolution*, Vol. 2, pp. 62–63, 150–72; Kennan, *Russia and the West*, pp. 65–116; Ullman, *Intervention and the War; Intervention, Civil War and Communism*, ed. John Bunyan (Baltimore: Johns Hopkins University Press, 1936); pp. 68–111, 277–303; John A. White, *The Siberian Intervention* (Princeton: Princeton University Press, 1950), esp. pp. 347–48; John Swettenham, *Allied Intervention in Russia, 1918–1919* (London: George Allen & Unwin, 1967), pp. 50–82, 92–136, 162–231, 243–44. R. Ernest Dupuy, *Perish by the Sword* (Harrisburg, Pa.: Military Service Publishing Company, 1939), and E. M. Halliday, *The Ignorant Armies* (New York: Award, 1964), provide excellent accounts of U.S. military operations in Russia; Robert Jackson, *At War with the Bolsheviks* (London: Tom Stacey, 1972), performs the same service for the British.

5. Fritz Fischer, *Germany's War Aims in the First World War* (New York: Norton, 1967), pp. 567–75.

6. Chamberlin, *The Russian Revolution*, Vol. 2, pp. 25–31, 44–45, 50–57, 67–80, 96–119; Schapiro, *Communist Party of the Soviet Union* 25–31, 44–45, 50–57, 67–80, 96–119; Roy Medvedev, *The October Revolution* (New York: Knopf, 1979), pp. 117–43, 182–84; Leonard Schapiro, *The Russian Revolutions of 1917* (New York: Basic Books, 1984), pp. 173–87, Keep, *The Russian Revolution*, pp. 306–462.

7. Carr, *The Bolshevik Revolution*, Vol. 1, p. 180; Schapiro, *Communist Party of the Soviet Union*, pp. 190–96; Leonard Schapiro, *The Origins of the Communist Autocracy* (Cambridge: Cambridge University Press, 1955), pp. 162, 191–208.

8. Chamberlin, *The Russian Revolution*, Vol. 2, pp. 18–20, 119–36, 172–80, 209–338; Kenez, *Civil War in South Russia, 1918*, pp. 169–271; Starikov and Medvedev, *Philip Mironov*, pp. 73–93; Lehovich, *White against Red*, pp. 228–40, 276–77, 281–82; Pipes, *The Formation of the Soviet Union*, pp. 133–43.

9. R. H. Ullman, *Britain and the Russian Civil War* (Princeton, NJ: Princeton University Press, 1968), esp. pp. 11–18, 60–97, 118–28, 132–33, 137–39, 215, 220–22, 278, 295–300, 332–33, 351, 360. Kennan, *Russia and the West*, pp. 118–43; Winston Churchill, *The Aftermath* (New York: Scribner's, 1929), pp. 164, 170–86, 243, 246–50, 254, 261–63, 265–71, 284–88.

10. Churchill, *The Aftermath*, p. 285.

11. Chamberlin, *The Russian Revolution*, Vol. 2, pp. 173–204, 209–219; Pipes, *The Formation of the Soviet Union*, pp. 162–63; Swettenham, *Allied Intervention in Russia*, pp. 182, 234–38.

12. William Rosenberg, *A. I. Denikin and the Anti-Bolshevik Movement in South Russia* (Amherst: Amherst College Press, 1961); Chamberlin, *The Russian Revolution*, Vol. 2, pp. 244–84; Peter Kenez, *Civil War in South Russia, 1919–1920* (Berkeley: University of California Press, 1977); Ullman, *Britain and the Russian Civil War*, pp. 212–13; Lehovich, *White against Red*, pp. 288–388.

13. Chamberlin, *The Russian Revolution*, Vol. 2, pp. 335–76, 430–49; Schapiro, *Communist Party of the Soviet Union*, pp. 190–235.

14. B. H. Liddell-Hart, *The Tanks* (London: Cassell,1959), pp. 212–13.

15. John M. Thompson, "Lenin's Analysis of Intervention," *American Slavic and East European Review* 17 (April 1958): 151–60; Ullman, *Britain and the Russian Civil War*, p. 321; Lehovich, *White against Red*, p. 340.

16. Churchill, *The Aftermath*, p. 235.

17. Ullman, *Intervention and the War*, p. 291 n 25; George F. Kennan, *The Decision to Intervene* (Princeton, NJ: Princeton University Press, 1958), pp. 106, 130, 153.

CHAPTER 4: THE RECONQUEST OF THE RUSSIAN EMPIRE

1. Pipes, *The Formation of the Soviet Union*, pp. 41–47, 108–111; Elliot Goodman , *The Soviet Design for a World State* (New York: Columbia University Press, 1960), pp. 211–33; Carr, *The Bolshevik Revolution*, Vol. 1, pp. 259–74.

2. Quoted in Page, *Lenin and World Revolution*, p. 121.

3. Page, *Lenin and World Revolution*, pp. 121–22; Chamberlin, *The Russian Revolution*, Vol. 2, pp. 207–208.

4. Lenin, *Sochineniya*, Vol. 24, p. 531.

5. Pipes, *The Formation of the Soviet Union*, pp. 175–89; Chamberlin, *The Russian Revolution*, Vol. 2, pp. 418–25; Bennigsen, "Conquest of the Moslem Borderlands," pp. 61–70; Page, *Lenin and World Revolution*, pp. 143–45.

6. Pipes, *The Formation of the Soviet Union*, pp. 195–97; 214–40; Chamberlin, *The Russian Revolution*, Vol. 2, pp. 406–417; Robert Tucker, *Stalin as Revolutionary* (New York: Norton, 1974), pp. 232–36.

7. Ulam, *The Bolsheviks*, pp. 484–85; Carr, *The Bolshevik Revolution*, Vol. 1, pp. 359–67.

CHAPTER 5: WORLD REVOLUTION

1. C. Jay Smith, "Soviet Russia and the Red Revolution of 1918 in Finland," in *The Anatomy of Communist Takeovers*, pp. 71–98; C. Jay Smith, *Finland and the Russian Revolution* (Athens, Ga.: University of Georgia Press, 1958), pp. 12–91; J. O. Hannula, *Finland's War of Independence* (London: Faber & Faber. 1939); Richard Luckett, *The White Generals* (New York: Viking, 1971), pp. 133–50.

2. Werner T. Angress, "The Takeover That Remained in Limbo," in *The Anatomy of Communist Takeovers*, pp. 163–74; Franz Borkenau, *World Communism* (Ann Arbor: University of Michigan Press, 1962), pp. 134–60; Page, *Lenin and World Revolution*, pp. 112–18; A. J. Ryder, *The German Revolution of 1918* (Cambridge: Cambridge University Press, 1967); Eric Waldman, *The Spartacist Rising of 1919* (Milwaukee: Marquette University Press, 1958); Arthur Rosenberg, *Imperial Germany* (Boston: Beacon, 1964), pp. 235–74; Carr, *The Bolshevik Revolution*, Vol. 3, pp. 82–86, 98–103, 111–16.

3. Borkenau, *World Communism*, pp. 108–133; Rudolf Tokes, *Bela Kun and the Hungarian Soviet Republic* (New York: Praeger, 1967); Helmut Gruber, *International Communism in the Era of Lenin* (Greenwich, Conn.: Fawcett, 1967), pp. 135–41; Peter Toma, "The Slovak Soviet Republic of 1919," *American Slavic and East European Review* 17 (April 1958): 203–215.

4. Carr, *The Bolshevik Revolution*, Vol. 3, pp. 123–53; Borkenau, *World Communism*, pp. 161–88; Page, *Lenin and World Revolution*, pp. 126–33.

5. Page, *Lenin and World Revolution*, pp. 141–45; Goodman, *The Soviet Design for a World State*, pp. 32–33. However, many authorities date this change only to mid-1920.

6. Quoted in Gruber, *International Communism in the Era of Lenin*, p. 227.

7. Page, *Lenin and World Revolution*, pp. 145–84; Carr, *The Bolshevik Revolution*, Vol. 3, pp. 181–85, 194–200, 253–60; Conrad Brandt, *Stalin's Failure in China* (New York: Norton, 1966), pp. 2–15; Allen S. Whiting, *Soviet Policies in China* (Stanford: Stanford University Press, 1968), pp. 36–58.

8. Chamberlin, *The Bolshevik Revolution*, Vol. 2, pp. 298–316; Carr, *The Bolshevik Revolution*, Vol. 3, pp. 213–16; Warren Lerner, "Attempting a Revolu-

tion from Without: Poland in 1920," in The Anatomy of Communist Takeovers, pp. 94–106.

9. Thomas T. Hammond, "The Communist Takeover of Outer Mongolia," in *The Anatomy of Communist Takeovers*, pp. 107–144; Carr, *The Bolshevik Revolution*, Vol. 3, pp. 506–509, 513–16.

10. Carr, *The Bolshevik Revolution*, Vol. 3, pp. 239–53, 290–301, 462–71; Adam Ulam, *Expansion and Coexistence* (New York: Praeger, 1968), pp. 121–25; Borkenau, *World Communism*, pp. 289–95. For a different interpretation of this issue see Helmut Gruber, *Soviet Russia Masters the Comintern* (New York: Anchor, 1974), esp. pp. 243–76.

11. Kennan, *Russia and the West Under Lenin and Stalin*, pp. 196–197.

12. Kennan, *Russia and the West*, pp. 164–226; Carr, *The Bolshevik Revolution*, Vol. 3, pp. 288–89, 339–80.

13. Interestingly, Allied operations against Nazi Germany in World War II presented a similar picture. Allied agencies had valuable contacts with anti-Nazi German officials but were unable to introduce agents from the outside until the very last part of the war. Then they used anti-Nazi German prisoners of war, but even these men did not accomplish much.

14. Walter Laqueur, *Russia and Germany* (Boston: Little, Brown, 1965), pp. 128–33; Paul Blackstock, *The Secret Road to World War II* (Chicago: Quadrangle, 1969), pp. 15–216; Gabriel Gorodetsky, *The Precarious Truce* (Cambridge: Cambridge University Press, 1977); Nigel West, *MI6* (New York: Random House, 1983), pp. 23–24, 27–32, 38–39; Gordon Brook-Shepherd, *The Storm Petrels* (New York: Ballantine, 1981); Chapman Pincher, *Too Secret, Too Long* (New York: St. Martin's Press, 1985), pp. 28–30; Ellen Hammer, *The Struggle for Indochina* (Stanford: Stanford University Press, 1955), p. 86.

15. Possony, *A Century of Conflict*, pp. 402–409; Selznick, *The Organizational Weapon*, pp. 114, 126–29, 144–50; Page, *Lenin and World Revolution*, pp. 188–99; Carew-Hunt, *The Theory and Practice of Communism*, pp. 195, 202–203; Carr, *The Bolshevik Revolution*, Vol. 3, pp. 386–87, 401–403.

16. Lenin, *Sochineniya*, Vol. 27, pp. 416–17; Goodman, *Soviet Design for a World State*, p. 188.

17. Angress, "The Takeover That Remained in Limbo," pp. 183–88; Borkenau, *World Communism*, pp. 238–53; Gruber, *International Communism*, pp. 412–17, 434–45; Anthony F. Upton, *Communism in Scandinavia* (New York: Anchor, 1973), p. 145; Jan Valtin (pseudonym of Richard Krebs), *Out of the Night* (New York: Alliance, 1941), pp. 41–86.

CHAPTER 6: STALINISM

1. Karel Kaplan, *Dans les archives du comité central: Trente ans de secretes du Bloc Sovietique* (Paris: Albin Michel, 1978), pp. 162–66; Boris

Nicolaevsky, *Power and the Soviet Elite* (New York: Praeger, 1965), p. 170.

2. Roy A. Medvedev, *Let History Judge: The Origins and Consequences of Stalinism*, Georges Haupt and David Joravsky, eds. (New York, 1973), pp. 329–30.

3. ·Milovan Djilas, *Conversations with Stalin* (New York: Harcourt Brace, 1962), pp. 190–91.

4. Robert Conquest, *The Great Terror* (New York: Collier, 1973), p. 111.

5. Kennan, *Russia and the West*, pp. 230–44; Schapiro, *Communist Party of the Soviet Union*, pp. 272–312; Tucker, *Stalin as Revolutionary*; Adam Ulam, *Stalin* (New York: Viking, 1973); Medvedev, *Let History Judge*, esp. pp. 325–30; Djilas, *Conversations with Stalin*.

6. Josef Stalin, *Problems of Leninism* (Moscow: Foreign Languages Publishing House, 1947), pp. 156–60; Carew-Hunt, *The Theory and Practice of Communism*, pp. 216–25; Goodman, *Soviet Design for a World State*, pp. 129–43; Schapiro, *Communist Party of the Soviet Union*, pp. 293–94; "Stalin's Letter to Comrade Ivanov," in *World Communism*, ed. Sidney Hook (Princeton: D. Van Nostrand, 1962), pp. 77–78.

7. Kermit McKenzie, *Comintern and World Revolution* (New York: Columbia University Press, 1964), p. 5.

8. Goodman, *Soviet Design for a World State*, p. 298.

9. Goodman, *Soviet Design for a World State*, p. 298; Schapiro, *Communist Party of the Soviet Union*, pp. 356, 362, 483; Stalin, *Sochineniya*, Vol. 7. (Moscow, 1947), p. 13–14; Stalin, *Problems of Leninism*, pp. 34–38, 94–124; 199; Possony, *A Century of Conflict*, pp. 127–37.

10. Possony, *A Century of Conflict*, pp. 138–48, 158–65; McKenzie, *Comintern and World Revolution*, pp. 55–57, 119–25.

CHAPTER 7: THE STRUGGLE FOR CHINA, 1924–1935

1. Michael Vyvyan, quoted in Geoffrey Fairbairn, *Revolutionary Guerilla Warfare* (New York: Penguin, 1974), p. 86.

2. Sidney Klein, *The Pattern of Land Tenure Reform in East Asia after World War II* (New York: Bookman, 1958); Hugh Seton-Watson, *From Lenin to Khrushchev* (New York: Praeger, 1960), pp. 111–23, 127–28, 130–34, 136–37; George E. Taylor, "Communism and Chinese History," in *Soviet and Chinese Communism: Similarities and Differences*, ed. Donald Treadgold (Seattle: University of Washington Press, 1967), pp. 24–36; Brandt, *Stalin's Failure in China*, pp. 27–29.

3. Brandt, *Stalin's Failure in China*, pp. 19ff; Robert C. North, *Moscow and Chinese Communists*, 2nd ed. (Stanford: Stanford University Press, 1963), pp. 42–121; Harold Isaacs, *The Tragedy of the Chinese Revolution*, 3rd ed. (Stan-

ford: Stanford University Press, 1961); Gottfried-Karl Kindermann, "The Attempted Revolution in China: The First Sino-Soviet Alliance, 1924–1927," in *The Anatomy of Communist Takeovers*, pp. 192–213.

4. Leslie Palmier, *Communists in Indonesia* (New York: Anchor, 1974), pp. 32–109; George Kahin, *Nationalism and Revolution in Indonesia* (Ithaca: Cornell University Press, 1952), pp. 71–87.

5. Richard C. Thornton, *China: The Struggle for Power* (Bloomington: Indiana University Press, 1973), pp. 25–58; Stuart Schram, *Mao Tse-tung* (New York: Penguin, 1968), pp. 131–55; Jerome Chen, *Mao and the Chinese Revolution* (New York: Oxford University Press, 1965), pp. 138–78; North, *Moscow and Chinese Communists*, pp. 122–60.

6. Lloyd Eastman, *The Abortive Revolution* (Cambridge: Harvard University Press, 1974), p. 205.

7. Eastman, *The Abortive Revolution*, esp. pp. 205, 216–17, 228, 239–43; Lloyd Eastman, *Seeds of Destruction* (Stanford: Stanford University Press, 1984), pp. 216–28; James L. Sheridan, *China in Disintegration* (New York: Free Press, 1975), esp. 22–23, 220–41.

8. Thornton, *China: The Struggle for Power*, pp. 58–81; North, *Moscow and Chinese Communists*, pp. 163–75; Schram, *Mao Tse-tung*, pp. 155–86; Chen, *Mao and the Chinese Revolution*, pp. 180–89.

CHAPTER 8: EUROPE IN THE 1930s

1. Laqueur, *Russia and Germany*, pp. 196–226, 229–32, 240–48; Borkenau, *World Communism*, pp. 338–356, 375–85; Franz Borkenau, *European Communism* (New York: Harper's, 1953), pp. 65–75; Eliot Wheaton, *Prelude to Calamity* (New York: Anchor, 1968), pp. 154–58; Gunther Nollau, *International Communism and Proletarian Revolution* (New York: Praeger, 1961), pp. 108–113; Max Beloff, *The Foreign Policy of Soviet Russia*, Vol. 1 (London: Oxford University Press, 1949), pp. 59–68; Possony, *A Century of Conflict*, pp. 196–206; Stefan Possony, "The Comintern as an Instrument of Soviet Strategy," in *The Revolutionary Internationals*, ed. Milorad Drachkovitch (Stanford: Hoover Institution Press, 1966), pp. 211–19; Raphael Abramovitch, *The Soviet Revolution* (New York: Universities Press, 1962), pp. 373–74.

2. James McSherry, *Stalin, Hitler and Europe*, Vol. 1 (Cleveland: World, 1968–70), pp. 21–66; Max Beloff, *The Foreign Policy of Soviet Russia*, Vol. 2 (London: Oxford University Press, 1949), pp. 4–26; Ulam, *Expansion and Coexistence*, pp. 182–232.

3. Georgi Dimitrov, *The United Front* (New York: International Publishers, 1938), pp. 89, 93; Selznick, *The Organizational Weapon*, pp. 129–33, 139–44;

McKenzie, *Comintern and World Revolution*, pp. 139–60, 164–65, 197, 206; Borkenau, *European Communism*, pp. 115–62.

4. Walter Krivitsky, *In Stalin's Secret Service* (New York: Harper's, 1939), pp. 2–24, 72–75, 225–36; Blackstock, *Secret Road to World War II*, pp. 282, 296–98; Abramovich, *The Soviet Revolution*, pp. 373, 406, 435–37; McSherry, *Stalin, Hitler and Europe*, Vol. 1, pp. 41–42, 51–52; *Documents on German Foreign Policy* Series C, Vol. 5 (Washington, D.C.: GPO, 1966), pp. 571–73, 931–33; Anton Antonov-Ovseeyenko, *The Time of Stalin* (New York: Harper & Row, 1980), p. 258; Brook-Shepherd, *The Storm Petrels*, pp. 142–77.

5. Conquest, *The Great Terror*; Blackstock, *Secret Road to World War II*, pp. 287–318; Stephen Cohen, *Bukharin and the Bolshevik Revolution* (New York: Vintage, 1973), pp. 359–62; Robert C. Tucker, *The Soviet Political Mind*, rev. ed. (New York: Norton, 1977), pp. 71–78; M. K. Dziemanowski, *The Communist Party of Poland* (Cambridge: Harvard University Press, 1959), pp. 149–54; Medvedev, *Let History Judge*, pp. 153–239.

6. Beloff, *The Foreign Policy of Soviet Russia*, Vol. 2, pp. 292–327; *Nazi-Soviet Relations* (Washington, D.C.: GPO, 1948), p. 147; *The Essential Stalin*, ed. H. Bruce Franklin (New York: Doubleday, 1974), pp. 324–36.

7. McSherry, *Stalin, Hitler and Europe*, Vol. 1, p. 109.

8. Gottfried Niedhart, "British Attitudes and Policies toward the Soviet Union," in *The Fascist Challenge and the Policy of Appeasement*, ed. Wolfgang Mommsen and Lothar Koettenoher (London: George Allen & Unwin, 1983), pp. 286–96; James Herndon, "British Perceptions of Soviet Military Capability," in ibid., pp. 297–316; Keith Middlemas, *The Strategy of Appeasement* (Chicago: Quadrangle, 1972), esp, pp. 52–53, 200; William Rock, *British Appeasement in the 1930s* (New York: Norton, 1977).

9. Borkenau, *European Communism*, pp. 182, 186, 192–98, 203–209, 217; Beloff, *The Foreign Policy of Soviet Russia*, Vol. 2, p. 199; Ulam, *Expansion and Coexistence*, pp. 227–29.

10. Stanley Payne, *The Spanish Revolution* (New York: Norton, 1970); Hugh Thomas, *The Spanish Civil War* (New York: MacMillan, 1961); Burnett Bolloten, *The Grand Camouflage* (New York: Praeger, 1961). For a version somewhat more favorable to the Republicans see Gabriel Jackson, *The Spanish Republic and Civil War* (Princeton, NJ: Princeton University Press, 1965).

11. Payne, *The Spanish Revolution*, pp. 157–270; Borkenau, *European Communism*, pp. 165–70.

12. Arthur Koestler, *The Invisible Writing* (New York: MacMillan, 1954), p. 326; Fitzroy Maclean, *Eastern Approaches* (New York: Atheneum, 1984), p. 13.

13. Bolloten, *The Grand Camouflage*, pp. 95–13, 120, 125, 129–31, 164–91, 201, 206, 223, 226–40, 272–316; Payne, *The Spanish Revolution*, pp. 268–368; Borkenau, *European Communism*, pp. 169–91; Conquest, *The Great Terror*, pp. 316, 588–92.

14. Gerhard Weinberg, *The Foreign Policy of Hitler's Germany: Starting World War II* (Chicago: University of Chicago Press, 1980), pp. 36–41; E. M. Robertson, *Hitler's Prewar Policy and Military Plans* (New York: Citadel, 1963), pp. 105–114, 125; Norman Rich, *Hitler's War Aims* (New York: Norton, 1973), pp. 97–99.

15. Beloff, The Foreign Policy of Soviet Russia, Vol. 2, pp. 120–36, 139–66; Weinberg, The Foreign Policy of Hitler's Germany, pp. 415–16; McSherry, Stalin, Hitler and Europe, Vol. 1, pp. 58–96; Josef Korbel, *Twentieth Century Czechoslovakia* (New York: Columbia University Press, 1977), pp. 137–43, 145.

16. Weinberg, *The Foreign Policy of Hitler's Germany*, pp. 503–504, 516, 533–34, 545; McSherry, *Stalin, Hitler and Europe*, Vol. 1, pp. 99–121.

17. *The Essential Stalin*, pp. 334–46; Beloff, *The Foreign Policy of Soviet Russia*, Vol. 2, pp. 221–23, 226–27. Cf. Ulam, *Expansion and Coexistence*, pp. 257–65.

18. Ulam, *Expansion and Coexistence*, pp. 265–73; McSherry, *Stalin, Hitler and Europe*, Vol. 1, pp. 164–99, 214–30; Weinberg, *The Foreign Policy of Hitler's Germany*, pp. 570–71, 612–14; Sidney Aster, *1939* (New York: Simon & Schuster, 1974), pp. 29ff.

19. Weinberg, *The Foreign Policy of Hitler's Germany*, pp. 570–629; McSherry, *Stalin, Hitler and Europe*, Vol. 1, pp. 146–63, 201–214; Aster, *1939*, pp. 296–97, 307ff.

CHAPTER 9: EAST ASIA: THE 1930s AND AFTER

1. James B. Crowley, *Japan's Quest for Autonomy* (Princeton: Princeton University Press, 1966), esp. pp. 294–97; Robert Butow, *Tojo and the Coming of the War* (Princeton: Princeton University Press, 1961), p. 83.

2. Chong-sik Lee, *Revolutionary Struggle in Manchuria* (Berkeley: University of California Press, 1982); Alvin Coox, *Nomonhan* (Stanford: Stanford University Press, 1985), pp. 11–70, 93–95.

3. Samuel B. Griffith, *The Chinese People's Liberation Army* (New York: McGraw-Hill, 1967), p. 58; Thornton, *China: The Struggle for Power*, pp. 90–103; Chen, *Mao and the Chinese Revolution*, pp. 201–204; *The Chinese Communist Movement* (Stanford: Stanford University Press, 1968), pp. 38–43; Schram, *Mao Tse-tung*, pp. 199–202; North, *Moscow and Chinese Communists*, pp. 178–80.

4. F. C. Jones, *Japan's New Order in East Asia* (London: Oxford University Press, 1954), pp. 173–85, 209; F. F. Liu, *A Military History of Modern China* (Princeton: Princeton University Press, 1956), pp. 168–70; Coox, *Nomonhan*; Martin Caidin, *The Ragged Rugged Warriors* (New York: Ballantine, 1967), pp. 102–110; North, *Moscow and Chinese Communists*, pp. 183–84; James C. Bowden, "Soviet Military Assistance to Nationalist China," in *Sino-Soviet*

Military Relations, Raymond Garthoff, ed. (New York: Praeger, 1966), pp. 44–56.

5. Arthur A. Cohen, *The Communists of Mao Tse-tung* (Chicago: University of Chicago Press, 1964); Raymond F. Wylie, *The Emergence of Mao Tse-tung* (Stanford: Stanford University Press, 1980); Chen, *Mao and the Chinese Revolution*, pp. 216–24; Schram, *Mao Tse-tung*, pp. 211, 224; Thornton, *China: The Struggle for Power*, pp. 105–121.

6. Martin Ebon, *Lin Piao* (New York: Stein & Day, 1970), pp. 25–27; Schram, *Mao Tse-tung*, pp. 208, 265n; Thornton, *China: The Struggle for Power*, pp. 104–107, 124, 133–37; Charles B. McLane, *Moscow and the Chinese Communists* (New York: Columbia University Press, 1958).

Communist sources loyal to the Soviet side in current disputes claim that as early as the Long March, Mao was disloyal to the Comintern line, seeking at various times to provoke war between the Soviet Union and the Nationalists or the Japanese, and attempting to pursue civil war instead of the Popular Front policy. See, for example, Otto Braun, *A Comintern Agent in China* (Stanford: Stanford University Press, 1982). These charges seem to refer to supposed intentions, rather than actions, and seem not to be susceptible to proof or disproof.

7. Chalmers Johnson, *Peasant Nationalism and Communist Power* (Stanford: Stanford University Press, 1962), pp. 2–4, 11, 19, 44, 70–77, 84–115; Griffith, *The Chinese People's Liberation Army*, pp. 62–68; *The Chinese Communist Movement*, pp. 45–55.

8. Johnson, *Peasant Nationalism and Communist Power*, pp. 136–40; Griffith, *The Chinese People's Liberation Army*, p. 69; *The Chinese Communist Movement*, pp. 67–87; Thornton, *China: The Struggle for Power*, pp. 105–107, 124.

9. Griffith, *The Chinese People's Liberation Army*, pp. 70–75; Johnson, *Peasant Nationalism and Communist Power*, pp. 31–72; *The Chinese Communist Movement*, pp. 110–22; Thornton, *China: The Struggle for Power*, p. 122.

CHAPTER 10: THE ERA OF THE NAZI-SOVIET PACT

1. Ulam, *Expansion and Coexistence*, pp. 280–83; McSherry, *Stalin, Hitler and Europe*, Vol. 1, pp. 242–47; ibid., Vol. 2, pp. 7–14; Edgar Tomson, "The Annexation of the Baltic States," in *The Anatomy of Communist Takeovers*, pp. 214–18.

2. Borkenau, *European Communism*, pp. 233–40, 297–300; Ulam, *Expansion and Coexistence*, pp. 233–40, 280–89, 297–300; Ulam, *Expansion and Coexistence*, pp. 280–289; Gabriel Almond, *The Appeals of Communism* (Princeton: Princeton University Press, 1954), p. 309.

3. Borkenau, *European Communism*, pp. 240–64, 300–305; Seton-Watson, *From Lenin to Khrushchev*, pp. 200–201; Alistair Horne, *To Lose a Battle* (New York: Penguin, 1979), pp. 145–47, Josef Korbel, *The Communist Subversion of Czechoslovakia* (Princeton: Princeton University Press, 1959), pp. 41–45.

4. McSherry, *Stalin, Hitler and Europe*, Vol. 2, p. 7; Beloff, *The Foreign Policy of Soviet Russia*, Vol. 2, pp. 290–96; Trumbull Higgins, *Hitler and Russia* (New York: MacMillan, 1966), pp. 37–54; Anthony Sokol, "The Cruise of Schiff 45," *United States Naval Proceedings* 77 (May 1951): 476–89.

5. McSherry, *Stalin, Hitler and Europe*, Vol. 2, pp. 23–89, 110–11; Beloff, *The Foreign Policy of Soviet Russia*, Vol. 2, pp. 305–310; Nikolai Tolstoy, *Stalin's Secret War* (New York: Norton, 1981), pp. 110, 129–64; Ulam, *Expansion and Coexistence*, pp. 290–95; Ulam, Stalin, p. 520; Medvedev, *Let History Judge*, p. 445.

6. Borkenau, *European Communism*, pp. 249–60, 305–312, 441; Henri Michel, *The Shadow of War* (New York: Doubleday, 1972), pp. 181–83; A. Rossi (Angelo Tasca), *A Communist Party in Action* (New Haven: Yale University Press, 1949), p. 14; Robert O. Paxton, *Vichy France* (New York: Norton, 1975), p. 14.

7. Tomson, "Annexation of the Baltic States," pp. 218–28; McSherry, *Stalin, Hitler and Europe*, Vol. 2, pp. 90–92, 97–110, 121–24; Ulam, *Expansion and Coexistence*, pp. 297–99.

8. McSherry, *Stalin, Hitler and Europe*, Vol. 2, pp. 143–201; Ulam, *Expansion and Coexistence*, pp. 304–305.

9. Higgins, *Hitler and Russia*, pp. 103–106, 135–36; McSherry, *Stalin, Hitler and Europe*, Vol. 2, pp. 205–238; Ulam, *Expansion and Coexistence*, pp. 306–312; Borkenau, *European Communism*, pp. 259–64, 347–50; J. B. Hoptner, *Yugoslavia in Crisis* (New York: Columbia University Press, 1962), pp. 237, 276; Albert Seaton, *The Russo-German War* (New York: Praeger, 1970), pp. 12–22. Cf. Barton Whaley, *Codeword Barbarossa* (Cambridge: MIT Press, 1973).

10. Svetlana Alliuleyva, *Only One Year* (New York, 1970), p. 382.

CHAPTER 11: DIVERSIONARY FORMULAS

1. James Burnham, *The War We Are In* (New Rochelle, NY: Arlington, 1967), p. 326.

2. Edwin O. Reischauer, *The United States and Japan* (New York: Viking, 1973), pp. 25–26.

3. *Foreign Relations of the United States, 1941*, Volume 1 (Washington, D.C.: PO, 1957), pp. 620–21. Cf. George Fischer, *Soviet Opposition to Stalin* (Cambridge: Harvard University Press, 1952).

4. Tolstoy, *Stalin's Secret War*, pp. 10, 34, 284–87; Koestler, *The Invisible Writing*, pp. 40–43; Conquest, *The Great Terror*, pp. 665–84; George Orwell,

Collected Essays, Journalism and Letters, Vol. 4, ed. Sonia Orwell and Ian Angus (New York: Harcourt Brace & Jovanovich, 1968), p. 15; Sidney Hook, *Political Power and Personal Freedom* (New York: Collier, 1962), pp. 222, 225–40; William O'Neill, *A Better World* (New York: Simon & Schuster, 1982); Paul Hollander, *Political Pilgrims* (New York: Oxford University Press, 1981).

5. Koestler, *The Invisible Writing*, pp. 200–201.

6. Richard Pipes, "Communism and Russian History," in *Soviet and Chinese Communism*, pp. 3–6.

7. Abramovitch, *The Soviet Revolution*, pp. 359–61; Bertram D. Wolfe, *An Ideology in Power* (New York: Stein & Day, 1969), pp. 377–94; Kennan, *Russia and the West*, pp. 164–65.

Bibliography

BOOKS

Abramovitch, Raphael. *The Soviet Revolution*. New York: Universities Press, 1962.

Alliuleyva, Svetlana. *Only One Year*. New York: Harper & Row, 1969.

Almond, Gabriel. *The Appeals of Communism*. Princeton, NJ: Princeton University Press, 1954.

Antonov-Ovseeyenko, Anton. *The Time of Stalin*. New York: Harper & Row, 1980.

Aster, Sidney. *1939*. New York: Simon & Schuster, 1974.

Barnett, Correlli. *The Collapse of British Power*. New York: Morrow, 1972.

Beloff, Max. *The Foreign Policy of Soviet Russia*. London: Oxford University Press, 1949.

Black, Cyril, and Thornton, Thomas, editors. *Communism and Revolution*. Princeton, NJ: Princeton University Press, 1964.

Black, Cyril, ed. *The Modernization of Russia and Japan*. New York: Free Press, 1975.

Blackstock, Paul. *The Secret Road to World War II*. Chicago: Quadrangle, 1969.

Blackwell, William. *The Industrialization of Russia*. New York: Crowell, 1970.

Bolloten, Burnett. *The Grand Camouflage*. New York: Praeger, 1961.

Borkenau, Franz. *European Communism*. New York: Harper's, 1953.

————. *World Communism*. Ann Arbor: University of Michigan Press, 1962.

Brandt, Conrad. *Stalin's Failure in China*. New York: Norton, 1966.

Braun, Otto. *A Comintern Agent in China*. Stanford: Stanford University Press, 1982.

Brook-Shepherd, Gordon. *The Storm Petrels*. New York: Ballantine, 1981.

Bunyan, John, ed. *Intervention, Civil War and Communism*. Baltimore: Johns Hopkins University Press, 1936.

Butow, Robert. *Tojo and the Coming of the War*. Princeton, NJ: Princeton University Press, 1961.

Caidin, Martin. *The Ragged Rugged Warriors*. New York: Ballantine, 1967.

Carew-Hunt, R. N. *The Theory and Practice of Communism*. Baltimore: Penguin, 1957.

Carr, E. H. *The Bolshevik Revolution*. 3 vols. Baltimore: Penguin, 1970.

Chamberlin, W. H. *The Russian Revolution*. 2 vols. New York: Grosset & Dunlap, 1965.

Charques, Richard. *The Twilight of Imperial Russia*. Oxford: Oxford University Press, 1958

Chen, Jerome. *Mao and the Chinese Revolution*. New York: Oxford University Press, 1965.

Churchill, Winston. *The Aftermath*. New York: Scribner's, 1929.

———. *The Unknown War*. New York: Scribner's 1931.

Cohen, Arthur A. *The Communism of Mao Tse-tung*. Chicago: University of Chicago Press, 1964.

Cohen, Stephen. *Bukharin and the Bolshevik Revolution*. New York: Vintage, 1973.

Conquest, Robert.. *The Great Terror*. New York: Collier, 1973.

Coox, Alvin. *Nomonhan*. Stanford: Stanford University Press, 1985.

Crowley, James B. *Japan's Quest for Autonomy*. Princeton: Princeton University Press, 1966.

Daniels, Robert V. *Red October*. New York: Scribner's, 1967.

Dimitrov, Georgi. *The United Front*. New York: International Publishers, 1938.

Djilas, Milovan. *Conversations with Stalin*. New York: Harcourt Brace, 1962.

Documents on German Foreign Policy, Series C. Volume V. Washington, D. C.: GPO, 1966.

Drachkovitch, Milorad, editor. *The Revolutionary Internationals*. Stanford: Hoover Institution Press, 1966.

Dupuy, R. Ernest. *Perish by the Sword*. Harrisburg, Pa.: Military Service Publishing Company, 1939.

Dziemanowski, M. K. *The Communist Party of Poland*. Cambridge, MA: Harvard University Press, 1959.

Eastman, Lloyd. *The Abortive Revolution*. Cambridge, MA: Harvard University Press, 1974.

———. *Seeds of Destruction*. Stanford: Stanford University Press, 1984.

Ebon, Martin. *Lin Piao*. New York: Stein & Day, 1970.

Fairbairn, Geoffrey. *Revolutionary Guerilla Warfare*. New York: Penguin, 1974.

Fedyshyn, Oleh. *Germany's Drive to the East and the Ukrainian Revolution*. New Brunswick: Rutgers University Press, 1971.

Fieldhouse, D. K. *The Colonial Empires.* New York: Delacorte, 1966.

———. *Economics and Empire.* Ithaca: Cornell University Press, 1973.

Fischer, Fritz. *Germany's War Aims in the First World War.* New York: Norton, 1967.

Fischer, George. *Soviet Opposition to Stalin.* Cambridge, MA: Harvard University Press, 1952.

Florinsky, Michael. *The End of the Russian Empire.* New York: Collier, 1961.

Foreign Relations of the United States, 1941. Volume 1. Washington, D.C.: GPO, 1957.

Franklin, H. Bruce, ed. *The Essential Stalin.* New York: Doubleday, 1974.

Gann, L. H., and Duignan, Peter. *Burden of Empire.* Stanford: Hoover Institution Press, 1967.

Garthoff, Raymond, ed. *Sino-Soviet Military Relations.* New York: Praeger, 1966.

Goodman, Elliot. *The Soviet Design for a World State.* New York: Columbia Universtiy Press, 1960.

Gorodetsky, Gabriel. *The Precarious Truce.* Cambridge, MA: Cambridge University Press, 1977.

Griffith, Samuel B. *The Chinese People's Liberation Army.* New York: Mc-Graw-Hill, 1967.

Gruber, Helmut. *International Communism in the Era of Lenin.* Greenwich, Conn.: Fawcett, 1967.

———. *Soviet Russia Masters the Comintern.* New York: Anchor, 1974.

Halliday, E. M. *The Ignorant Armies.* New York: Award, 1964.

Hammer, Ellen. *The Struggle for Indochina.* Stanford: Stanford University Press, 1955.

Hammond, Thomas T., ed. *The Anatomy of Communist Takeovers.* New Haven: Yale University Pres, 1975.

Hannula, J. O. Finland's War of Independence. London: Faber & Faber, 1939.

Hart, B. H. Liddell. *The Tanks.* London: Cassell, 1959.

Higgins, Trumbull. *Hitler and Russia.* New York: MacMillan, 1966.

Hollander, Paul. *Political Pilgrims. New York: Oxford University Press, 1981.*

Hook, Sidney. *Marx and the Marxists.* Princeton, NJ: D. Van Nostrand, 1955.

———. *Political Power and Personal Freedom.* New York: Collier, 1962.

———. *World Communism.* Princeton, NJ: D. Van Nostrand, 1962.

Hoptner, J. B. *Yugoslavia in Crisis.* New York: Columbia University Press, 1962.

Horne, Alistair. *To Lose a Battle.* New York: Penguin, 1979.

Huntington, Samuel. *Political Order in Changing Societies.* New Haven, CT: Yale University Press, 1968.

Isaacs, Harold. *The Tragedy of the Chinese Revolution.* 3rd edition. Stanford: Stanford University Press, 1961.

Jackson, Gabriel. *The Spanish Republic and Civil War*. Princeton, NJ: Princeton University Press, 1965.

Jackson, Robert. *At War with the Bolsheviks*. London: Tom Stacey, 1972.

Jasny, Naum. *Soviet Industrialization*. Chicago: University of Chicago Press, 1961.

Johnson, Chalmers. *Autopsy on People's War*. Berkeley: University of California Press, 1973.

———. *Peasant Nationalism and Communist Power*. Stanford: Stanford University Press, 1962.

Jones, F. C. *Japan's New Order in East Asia*. London: Oxford University Press, 1954.

Kahin, George. *Nationalism and Revolution in Indonesia*. Ithaca, NY: Cornell University Press, 1952.

Kaplan, Karel. *Dans les archives du comite central: Trente ans de secretes du Bloc Sovietique*. Paris: Albin Michel, 1978.

Keep, John. *The Russian Revolution*. New York: Norton, 1976.

Kennan, George F. *The Decision to Intervene*. Princeton, NJ: Princeton University Press, 1958.

———. *Russia and the West under Lenin and Stalin*. New York: New American Library, 1962.

Koestler, Arthur. *The Invisible Writing*. New York: MacMillan, 1954.

Kenez, Peter. *Civil War in South Russia, 1918*. Berkeley: University of California Press, 1971.

———. *Civil War in South Russia, 1919–1920*. Berkeley: University of California Press, 1977.

Klein, Sidney. *The Pattern of Land Tenure Reform in East Asia after World War II*. New York: Bookman, 1958.

Korbel, Josef. *The Communist Subversion of Czechoslovakia*. Princeton, NJ: Princeton University Press, 1959.

———. *Twentieth Century Czechoslovakia*. New York: Columbia University Press, 1977.

Krivitsky, Walter. *In Stalin's Secret Service*. New York: Harper's, 1939.

Langer, William. *The Diplomacy of Imperialism*. Cambridge, MA: Harvard University Press, 1935.

Laqueur, Walter. *Russia and Germany*. Boston: Little, Brown, 1965.

Lee, Chong-sik. *Revolutionary Struggle in Manchuria*. Berkeley: University of California Press, 1982.

Lehovich, Dimitri V. *White against Red*. New York: Norton, 1974.

Lenin, V. I. *Sochineniya*. Moscow: 1930–35.

Liu, F. F. *A Military History of Modern China*. Princeton: Princeton University Press, 1956.

Luckett, Richard. *The White Generals*. New York: Viking, 1971.

McKenzie, Kermit. *Comintern and World Revolution.* New York: Columbia University Press, 1964.

Maclean, Fitzroy. *Eastern Approaches.* New York: Atheneum, 1984.

McLane, Charles B. *Moscow and the Chinese Communists.* New York: Columbia University Press, 1958.

McSherry, James. *Stalin, Hitler and Europe.* 2 vols. Cleveland, OH: World, 1968–70.

Medvedev, Roy. *Let History Judge.* New York: Vintage, 1973.

————. *The October Revolution.* New York: Knopf, 1979.

Melgunov, S. P. *The Bolshevik Seizure of Power.* Santa Barbara, Calif.: ABC Books, 1972.

Michel, Henri. *The Shadow War.* New York: Doubleday, 1972.

Middlemas, Keith. *The Strategy of Appeasement.* Chicago: Quadrangle, 1972.

Mommsen, Wolfgang, and Koettenoher, Lothar, eds. *The Fascist Challenge and the Policy of Appeasement.* London: George Allen & Unwin, 1983.

Nazi-Soviet Relations. Washington, D.C.: GPO, 1948.

Nicolaevsky, Boris. *Power and the Soviet Elite.* New York: Praeger, 1965.

Nollau, Gunther. *International Communism and Proletarian Revolution.* New York: Praeger, 1961.

North, Robert C. *Moscow and Chinese Communists.* 2nd edition. Stanford: Stanford University Press, 1963.

O'Neill, William. *A Better World.* New York: Simon & Schuster, 1982.

Orwell, George. *Collected Essays, Journalism and Letters.* Volume IV. New York: Harcourt Brace Jovanovich. 1968.

Padover, Saul. *Karl Marx.* New York: McGraw-Hill, 1978.

Page, Stanley. *Lenin and World Revolution.* New York: McGraw-Hill, 1972.

Palmier, Leslie. *Communists in Indonesia.* New York: Anchor, 1974.

Payne, Stanley. *The Spanish Revolution.* New York: Norton, 1970.

Paxton, Robert O. *Vichy France.* New York: Norton, 1975.

Pincher, Chapman. *Too Secret, Too Long.* New York: St. Martin's Press, 1985.

Pipes, Richard. *The Formation of the Soviet Union.* Revised edition. Cambridge, MA: Harvard University Press, 1964.

Poliakov, Leon. *The Aryan Myth.* New York: New American Library, 1977.

Possony, Stefan T. *A Century of Conflict.* Chicago: Regnery, 1953.

————. *The Lenin Reader.* Chicago: Regnery, 1966.

Reischauer, Edwin O. *The United States and Japan.* New York: Viking, 1973.

Rich, Norman. *Hitler's War Aims.* New York: Norton, 1973.

Robertson, E. M. *Hitler's Prewar Policy and Military Plans.* New York: Citadel, 1963.

Rock, William. *British Appeasement in the 1930s.* New York: Norton, 1977.

Rosenberg, Arthur. *Imperial Germany.* Boston: Beacon, 1964.

Rossi, A. (Angelo Tasca). *A Communist Party in Action.* New Haven: Yale University Press, 1949.

Rosenberg, William. *A. I. Denikin and the Anti-Bolshevik Movement in South Russia.* Amherst: Amherst College Press, 1961.

Rostow, Walt W. *Stages of Economic Growth.* Cambridge: Cambridge University Press, 1960.

Ryder, A. J. *The German Revolution of 1918.* Cambridge: Cambridge University Press, 1967.

Schapiro, Leonard. *The Communist Party of the Soviet Union.* New York: Vintage, 1969.

———. *The Origins of the Communist Autocracy.* Cambridge: Cambridge University Press, 1955.

———. *The Russian Revolutions of 1917.* New York: Basic Books, 1984.

Schram, Stuart. *Mao Tse-tung.* New York: Penguin, 1968.

Seaton, Albert. *The Russo-German War.* New York: Praeger, 1970.

Selznick, Philip. *The Organizational Weapon.* Glencoe, NY: Free Press, 1960.

Seton-Watson, Hugh. *From Lenin to Khrushchev.* New York: Praeger, 1960.

———. *The Imperialist Revolutionaries.* Stanford: Hoover Institution Press, 1978.

———. *The Russian Empire.* New York: Praeger, 1967.

Sheridan, James L. *China in Disintegration.* New York: Free Press, 1975.

Smith, C. Jay. *Finland and the Russian Revolution.* Athens, Ga.: University of Georgia Press, 1958.

Stalin, Josef. *Problems of Leninism.* Moscow: Foreign Languages Publishing House, 1947.

———. *Sochineniya.* Moscow, 1947.

Starikov, Sergei, and Medvedev, Roy. *Philip Mironov and the Russian Civil War.* New York: Knopf, 1978.

Stone, Norman. *The Eastern Front.* New York: Scribner's, 1975.

Swettenham, John. *Allied Intervention in Russia, 1918–1919.* London: George Allen & Unwin, 1967.

Thomas, Hugh. *The Spanish Civil War.* New York: MacMillan, 1961.

Thornton, Richard C. *China: The Struggle for Power.* Bloomington: Indiana University Press, 1973.

Tokes, Rudolf. *Bela Kun and the Hungarian Soviet Republic.* New York: Praeger, 1967.

Tolstoy, Nikolai. *Stalin's Secret War.* New York: Norton, 1981.

Treadgold, Donald. *Lenin and His Rivals.* New York: Praeger, 1955.

Tucker, Robert C. The Marxian Revolutionary Idea. New York: Norton, 1969.

———. *The Soviet Political Mind.* Revised edition. New York: Norton, 1977.

———. *Stalin as Revolutionary.* New York: Norton, 1974.

Ulam, Adam. *The Bolsheviks.* New York: Collier, 1968.
———. *Expansion and Coexistence.* New York: Praeger, 1968.
———. *Stalin.* New York: Viking, 1973.
Ullman, R. H. *Britain and the Russian Civil War.* Princeton, NJ: Princeton University Press, 1968.
———. *Intervention and the War.* Princeton, NJ: Princeton University Press, 1961.
Upton, Anthony F. *Communism in Scandinavia.* New York: Anchor, 1973.
Valtin, Jan (pseudonym of Richard Krebs.) *Out of the Night.* New York: Alliance, 1941.
Van Slyke, Lyman, editor. *The Chinese Communist Movement.* Stanford: Stanford University Press, 1968.
Waldman, Eric. *The Spartacist Rising of 1919.* Milwaukee, WI: Marquette University Press, 1958.
Weinberg, Gerhard. *The Foreign Policy of Hitler's Germany: Starting World War II.* Chicago: University of Chicago Press, 1980.
West, Nigel. *MI6.* New York: Random House, 1983.
Whaley, Barton. *Codeword Barbarossa.* Cambridge: MIT Press, 1973.
Wheaton, Eliot. *Prelude to Calamity.* New York: Anchor, 1968.
White, John A. *The Siberian Intervention.* Princeton, NJ: Princeton University Press, 1950.
Whiting, Allen S. *Soviet Policies in China.* Stanford: Stanford University Press, 1968.
Wolfe, Bertram D. *An Ideology in Power.* New York: Stein & Day, 1969.
———. *Three Who Made a Revolution.* New York: Dial, 1948.
Wylie, Raymond F. *The Emergence of Mao Tse-tung.* Stanford: Stanford University Press, 1980.
Zeman, Z. A. B. *Germany and the Russian Revolution.* Oxford: Oxford University Press, 1958.

ARTICLES

Angress, Werner T. "The Takeover That Remained in Limbo." In *The Anatomy of Communist Takeovers*, pp. 163–91. Edited by Thomas T. Hammond. New Haven, CT: Yale University Press, 1975.
Bennigsen, Alexandre. "The Conquest of the Moslem Borderlands." In *The Anatomy of Communist Takeovers*, pp. 61–70. Edited by Thomas T. Hammond. New Haven: Yale University Press, 1975.
Bowden, James C. "Soviet Military Assistance to Nationalist China." In *Sino-Soviet Military Relations*, pp. 44–56. Edited by Raymond Garthoff. New York: Praeger, 1966.

Hammond, Thomas T. "The Communist Takeover of Outer Mongolia." *In The Anatomy of Communist Takeovers*, pp. 107–144. Edited by Thomas T. Hammond. New Haven: Yale University Press, 1975.

Herndon, James. "British Perceptions of Soviet Military Capability." In *The Fascist Challenge and the Policy of Appeasement*, pp. 297–316. Edited by Wolfgang Mommsen and Lothar Koettenoher. London: George Allen & Unwin, 1983.

Kindermann, Gottfried-Karl. "The Attempted Revolution in China: The First Sino-Soviet Alliance, 1924–1927." In *The Anatomy of Communist Takeovers*, pp. 192–213. Edited by Thomas T. Hammond. New Haven: Yale University Press, 1975.

Lerner, Warren. "Attempting a Revolution from Without: Poland in 1920."In *The Anatomy of Communist Takeovers*, pp. 94–106. Edited by Thomas T. Hammond. New Haven: Yale University Press, 1975.

Niedhart, Gottfried. "British Attitudes and Policies Toward the Soviet Union." In *The Fascist Challenge and the Policy of Appeasement*, pp. 286–296. Edited by Wolfgang Mommsen and Lothar Koettenoher. London: George Allen & Unwin, 1983.

Pipes, Richard. "Communism and Russian History." *In Soviet and Chinese Communism: Similarities and Differences*, pp. 3–23. Edited by Donald Treadgold. Seattle, WA: University of Washington Press, 1967.

Possony, Stefan T. "The Comintern as an Instrument of Soviet Strategy." In *The Revolutionary Internationals*, pp. 211–19. Edited by Milorad Drachkovitch. Stanford: Hoover Institution Press, 1966.

Smith, C. Jay. "Soviet Russia and the Red Revolution of 1918 in Finland." In *The Anatomy of Communist Takeovers*, pp. 71–93. Edited by Thomas T. Hammond. New Haven: Yale University Press, 1975.

Sokol, Anthony. "The Cruise of Schiff 45." *United States Naval Institute Proceedings* 78 (May 1951): 476–89.

Taylor, George E. "Communism and Chinese History." In *Soviet and Chinese Communism: Similarities and Differences*, pp. 24–36. Edited by Donald Treadgold. Seattle: University of Washington Press, 1967.

Thompson, John M. "Lenin's Analysis of Intervention." *American Slavic and East European Review* 17 (April 1958): 151–60.

Toma, Peter. "The Slovak Soviet Republic of 1919." *American Slavic and East European Review* 17 (April 1958): 203–215.

Tomson, Edgar. "The Annexation of the Baltic States." In *The Anatomy of Communist Takeovers*, pp. 214–28. Edited by Thomas T. Hammond. New Haven: Yale University Press, 1975.

Index

About the Author

ALAN J. LEVINE is an historian specializing in Russian history and the study of twentieth-century international relations. Born and raised in New York City, he received a Ph.D. from New York University. Mr. Levine has worked as a teacher, freelance writer, and book reviewer. He has published numerous articles about World War II and the Cold War, and is currently completing a history of the Cold War from the surrender of Japan to the death of Josef Stalin.